GET TO KNOW
RON MARTIN

These endorsements come from people who know Ron Martin. Here's what they have to say about Ron, his selling system and his book,

Retail Selling Made Easy...

"Following the success of his first book, **Success Made Easy**, Ron Martin has put his talent to work on another great book. Every retailer should read and practice the nine easy steps that Ron proposes. I guarantee retail sales will experience a boost never before thought possible.

I only wish that I had met Ron earlier in my own career as a retailer. Now, as President of Retail Merchants of Hawaii, the best thing I can do is encourage all fellow retailers to take advantage of the wisdom and knowledge shared in this book.

We all have a responsibility to train and assist our sales force. Ron Martin has outlined an easy way to do that. The book is written in an easy-to-follow format with key concepts highlighted in each chapter.

Ron has proven his nine-step system in the marketplace working with hundreds of companies to perfect and teach **Retail Selling Made Easy.**

Put this book in your own library and give one to all your team members. Success is just around the corner. It's easy."

– Jan Berman
President
Retail Merchants of Hawaii

"Ron Martin has single-handedly changed the face of retail in Hawaii. This book gives his system to the rest of the world."

– Wyland
Environmental Artist

"We've had a 1000% increase in sales since Ron Martin brought his Pro-Active, No-Pressure Selling System into my business. We now sell in three days what we used to sell in a month. It *is* easy."

— MICHAEL FIEMAN
Owner, Loco Boutique
Hawaii-Guam-Japan

"Windward Mall has definitely benefitted from the teachings of Ron Martin. He has worked with our store owners and their salespeople conducting Success Rallies at the mall. His concerted efforts have resulted in our participating merchants experiencing incremental increases in sales over the prior year. In the austere times Hawaii has suffered from for more than three years, keeping our head above water is something to boast about."

— SANDI HAUNANI OGUMA
Marketing Director
Windward Mall
Bishop Estate

"**Retail Selling Made Easy** is not only enjoyable and easy to read, but the inspiration it creates can be translated into many different facets of doing business today, either directly with the public or indirectly with employees. It is a reflection of Ron's humor and spirit."

— CRAWFORD F. SHERMAN
Resident Manager
Mauna Lani Bay Hotel and Bungalows
Five Diamond Award

"As the head of a rapidly growing retail company, I am impressed with the results we have attained by following Ron Martin's nine-step system and principles as laid out in **Retail Selling Made Easy**. This book is a necessity for retailers in any stage of development."

— **Brick Thompson**
CEO
Business Management Co. Ltd.
Las Vegas, Nevada

"Ron Martin's nine-step selling system has been incredibly successful. This system helped Wyland Galleries grow from less than $1 million to more than $20 million in annual sales. I highly recommend **Retail Selling Made Easy** to *any* sales organization. Everyone deserves success."

– BILL WYLAND
Owner
Wyland Galleries-Hawaii

"Ron Martin's books and Success Rallies give one the opportunity to clearly understand and realize that we all have positive qualities we might not always use. Ron Martin explains how to use these qualities, and focus them towards success in a way that is understandable and fun. Follow this system, and you shall succeed; I did!"

– TAO MILLER
President
Body & Soul
Hawaii's 1995 Young Entrepreneur of the Year

"I love this book. It's not only **Retail Selling Made Easy,** but it is also made *fun.*"

– GUILLAUME MAMAN
Director of Stores
BEBE Sports-Honolulu
Previously Sales Manager
Louis Vuitton-Hawaii

"We have religiously used Ron's Pro-Active, No-Pressure Selling System in all of our stores for many years. We have achieved increased sales along with higher employee morale and motivation. We recommend Ron's system for *all* retail businesses."

– STEVE POGNI
Owner
Treasures Jewelry
California-Hawaii

"Ron's book arrived at a great time for me. This book made it *easy* for me to train eight new sales people in the art of selling. Ron's nine-step system gives all salespeople the tools they need to be successful. In our first three weeks my top salesperson had sales of $50,000 and when asked about his success he said, 'I just followed Ron Martin's nine steps.' It works!"

— **ANN FRANZMANN**
President
Wyland Gallery of Las Vegas

"Location • Location • Location — usually meant instant success in retail. However with the current worldwide economy, the best trained *salespeople* must be *selling* in those locations.

We use Ron Martin's nine-step system to help close sales, and continue to increase our average sale. This system has benefited our seasoned and new employees for many years. **Retail Selling Made Easy** is a must for all salespeople, sales trainers and store owners."

— **JIM GEIGER**
President
Waikiki Trader Corporation
Hawaii-Guam-Mainland U.S.A.

"In a struggling economy, where businesses were closing down all around us, the help and business expertise of Ron Martin provided the assistance we needed to pull through the hard times. *Now* we set new sales records every month."

— **HOWARD KONRAD**
Owner
Lahaina Scrimshaw
Jessica's Gems

RETAIL SELLING MADE EASY

RETAIL SELLING MADE EASY

RON MARTIN

Copyright © 1996 by Ron Martin

All rights reserved. No part of this book may be reproduced or utilized in any form or by any electronic or mechanical means, including photocopying, recording or by any information storage and retrieval system, without permission in writing from the publisher, except by a reviewer who may quote brief passages in a review. Inquires should be addressed to Success Dynamics, Inc., P.O. Box 489, Haleiwa, Hawaii 96712

Library of Congress Catalog Card Number: 96-092697

First Printing 1996

10 9 8 7 6 5 4 3 2

Printed in the United States of America

*In memory of my father Granville,
my wife Sarah, and my mother Frances.
All three left this earth a better place and while
here touched me as no others did or will.
Mahalo*

Contents

	Foreword by Doug Smoyer		i
Chapter 1	Selling Retail		1
Chapter 2	Selling Paradigms		5
Chapter 3	Selling Systematically		11
Chapter 4	Selling Yourself	Step 1	25
Chapter 5	Selling Silently	Step 2	37
Chapter 6	Selling Openers	Step 3	47
Chapter 7	Selling The Discovery	Step 4	55
Chapter 8	Selling Specifics	Step 5	65
Chapter 9	Selling Objections	Step 6	79
Chapter 10	Selling Decisions	Step 7	93
Chapter 11	Selling More	Step 8	101
Chapter 12	Selling Friendship	Step 9	109
Chapter 13	Selling Success Traits		115
Chapter 14	Selling Habits		125
Chapter 15	Selling with "The Boss"		133
Chapter 16	Selling Success		147
	Acknowledgements		149
	Book Ordering Information		152

Foreword

by Doug Smoyer
President, Retail Strategies Inc.

Ron Martin knows how to sell himself. Therefore, he is very good at teaching other people how to sell themselves *and* feel good about themselves. If you feel good about yourself, you have the number one quality to be a great salesperson.

Ron Martin knows how to motivate people. When you sit down with him in even casual conversation, you leave the table wanting to add another dimension to your life.

This book puts these talents of Ron's into a form that is accessible to anyone. Following the principles and system laid out in the chapters ahead will allow anyone to succeed in retail.

It has been said that retail success is location, location, location. Ron has demonstrated through his years of successful results in retail that truly great success can be achieved only through finely tuned and motivated *salespeople*.

Retail Selling Made Easy presents a system that will bring positive *results* in any retail store. The principles outlined apply to all categories of salespeople and products anywhere in the world.

Ron's first book, **Success Made Easy**, rose quickly to the top of Hawaii's non-fiction best sellers' list. **Retail Selling Made Easy** will enjoy even greater acclaim.

This book is a *must read* for all retailers who believe in servicing their customers and maximizing their business success.

Share this book with every member of your organization. **It's easy.**

Chapter 1

Selling Retail

*Retail: "To sell in small quantities
directly to the consumer..."*
WEBSTER

Retail selling *is* easy. Your customers walk in the door. In contrast, wholesale or direct salespeople must *find* a customer, then make the sale.

Salesmanship is essential in outside sales, and everyone knows it. High commissions and extensive training stimulate wholesale and direct salespeople to get out there and "sell, sell, sell." Books and seminars promote topics such as "getting past the secretary" and "closing the sale."

Because of the obstacles and the high rewards, many *direct* salespeople become pro-active and "high pressure" in their approach. This, unfortunately, has given *"selling"* a bad name. "Have you heard the one about the traveling salesman who...?"

My first sales experience was in *direct sales*. I owned Empress Pearls Inc., a home party jewelry sales company, with two partners in early 1966. We were the first company to sell high-quality, high-priced 14K jewelry in the home.

We started on a small table in my house, with an even smaller budget. A professional baseball player later invested $7,000 in our enterprise. That allowed us to expand our operations into my partner's garage.

In fifteen years we grew into a 20,000-square-foot jewelry factory on Hollywood Boulevard in Los Angeles with 100 employees and 5,000 independent salespeople, selling more than a million dollars of jewelry a month. We had 40 sales offices from New York to Hawaii. It was fun. **It was easy.**

In 1981, I sold my interest in the company to one of my partners and "retired" to Hawaii. After three months of surfing and playing, I was enticed into *retail*.

Waikiki is a retailer's paradise, with millions of tourists going from store to store, buying souvenirs and gifts to take back to the U. S. mainland, Europe and the Orient.

After devoting 15 years to "looking for customers," *retail* selling looked as easy as "shooting fish in a barrel." I dove in and helped increase one company's sales from $2 million to $24 million annually in just 10 years. It was the *easiest* success I had ever enjoyed.

I discovered that all retailers were not as fortunate as me. Surprisingly, many retailers struggle and fail in this rich Waikiki shopping environment.

 **Retailers fail every day in the face of great opportunity.**

My *direct selling* background gave me an appreciation for *salesmanship* that made my stores stand out among competing retailers.

By applying pro-active, no-pressure selling techniques we made our stores #1 in square footage sales in almost every retail center we operated. **It was easy.**

Today I am retained as a "Sales Resultant" by hundreds of retailers and shopping centers throughout Hawaii and the mainland to teach my Pro-Active, No-Pressure Selling System. It works. **It's easy.**

 **At Loco Boutique in Waikiki, sales increased 1,000% using Pro-Active, No-Pressure Selling.**

The success of a retail store depends mostly upon these factors:

1. Location
2. Merchandise
3. Salespeople

All too often, well-meaning, "wanna-be" retailers invest a fortune on location and merchandise, yet take the salespeople for granted.

Retailers may spend hundreds of thousands, even millions, of dollars to get the ideal location. Then they spend hundreds of thousands more on architects, contractors, fixtures and displays.

By the time they buy merchandise for the beautiful showcases in their ideal location, they have invested millions of dollars and haven't seen their first customer. Finally, they hire a staff.

They expect their good location, heavy traffic and desirable merchandise to do the selling job, so they hire untrained *clerks* at the smallest salary possible to merely "ring up" the sales.

Too often, some of these entrepreneurs face a rude awakening. Of the three necessary ingredients for retail success, they have underestimated the most important element: Salespeople.

Three Elements of Retail Success

1. **Location** - Every commercial Realtor will tell you that retail success depends upon three things: Location, location, location. That's not true. People fail every day in the best locations, and succeed in the poorest.

2. **Merchandise** - You don't need the *best* merchandise or the *best* prices to succeed. You need *good* merchandise and *fair* prices. Outstanding merchandise at great prices sits on store shelves in some fabulous locations, waiting to be *sold*.

3. **Salespeople** - Poor salespeople can make a good product fail in a great location. On the other hand, great salespeople can make an *average* product succeed in a *marginal* location. It happens every day.

Chapter 2

Selling Paradigms

Many people say, "I could never sell anything."

If you were asked to define selling, how would you? Think about it for a moment, then write your definition on a piece of paper. Look at it and analyze your words. This is important because your personal definition of selling creates a framework for your behavior as a salesperson.

The most common definition that people give to selling is: "Convincing people to buy something." Some say, "Selling is *talking people into* buying something."

The dictionary definition according to Webster is: "To transfer property in return for money or something else of value."

A young woman working in an art gallery once told me, "Selling is putting things off on people."

How you "see" your job determines how you *do* your job. I asked this young art consultant:

"How do you feel about *putting things off on* people?"

"Not very good," she replied.

"So why did you take this job?", I asked.

"Because I need the money," she said.

She will probably fail. Most people will not sacrifice their personal values or beliefs for money. This art consultant will go through the motions of selling, and *take* the money, but she will *not* "put things off on people." She has taken a job that, by her own definition, she cannot, or will not, do.

My advice to her was: *"Change your attitude or change your address."* To be successful, she must find a job she feels good about, *or* change her definition of selling into something she can feel good about.

Look at the first word in *your* definition of selling. Is it a *taking* word or a *giving* word? If your goal is to take people's money you will not be as successful as someone whose goal is to *give* something.

 **Selling is a *giving* profession, not a taking one.**

To sell is to *give.* Those who *give...* get. You *give* service and information. Your customers *give* you their money; you don't have to take it.

Thieves take money; salespeople earn it. **Selling is *giving* the customer sufficient information to make an intelligent buying decision, be it *yes* or *no*.**

If you believe you must get your customer's money in order to be successful, then you are setting yourself up for failure.

Salespeople who feel they must get the money to succeed often resort to pressure, becoming pushy and obnoxious. They succumb to using high pressure tactics whenever they sense rejection, disappointment or failure.

Salespeople who set goals to *give* information will succeed. You can always *give* information. **It's easy**.

When sufficient information is given, the customer can make an intelligent buying decision. Without sufficient information, the customer must make a purely emotional or impulsive buying decision.

 **Customers sold with *good information* become salespeople for your products or services. They return more often and refer you to their friends.**

It's a **"give/give"** and **"win/win"** experience.

Many retail salespeople ask: "If customers need information, why don't they ask?" and "Why do they try to avoid me?"

Customers react to their paradigms of salespeople. Paradigms are formed by years of personal experiences. A paradigm is a model or pattern of behavior you expect based on your experience.

Unfortunately, customers who have been intimidated by "pushy" salespeople will anticipate the same from you. As a result, customers act defensively when entering your store.

If customers fear you, they will try to avoid you, even though they need you. Such a customer's attitude is: "When I want your help, I'll ask for it."

All customers need your help. They need information. Your customers don't fear information, but they may fear *you*. This is why you must make the "trust sale" before you begin to make the product sale. The "trust sale" is not automatic.

 **People "buy people" before they buy merchandise.**

It's human nature. If you trust the salesperson, you trust what he or she sells, and vice versa. A sale is made or lost in the first seven seconds.

It's a sad scenario to see a business person invest a great deal of time and money, only to fail in the first seven seconds.

Deep-pocket, big box, multi-national retailers attempt to make the "trust sale" with huge advertising budgets that create a "feel good" image. Then they hire "clerks" to stock the shelves, and collect the money. These retailers have no idea how much more business they could do with real *salespeople*.

A customer who enters your store and announces, "I'm just looking," can paralyze you. Your job as a professional salesperson is to give needed information. If you allow your customers to "just look," then you fail to do your job.

On the other hand, if you force-feed information to your customers against their will, you fail too. Catch 22? No!

 **Customers "just looking" in your store also have an interest in, or a need for, what you sell.**

People who "just look" in an auto parts store probably work on cars or need to buy an auto part. Someone who walks into a tropical fish store is a collector, or is interested in tropical fish. Art collectors and art enthusiasts visit art galleries. People who wear jewelry go to jewelry stores, and people looking for clothes go to clothing stores. An exception would be people who are shopping for a gift.

Think about it: "just looking" is a lie. "*Buyers are liars.*" Customers lie to protect themselves from the very person they need the most: you!

I said that "just looking" is a lie; let me clarify that. It's only a *half*-lie. Customers *are* looking, but not *just* looking. They are looking for a gift, or for something to buy for themselves. They are not *just* looking. They are also walking, breathing and thinking.

With the proper approach, they will open up to you, ask questions, welcome your information, and buy.

If you believe, "just looking," and turn your back, their lies will come true. They will leave with nothing. Your customers will walk out without your information *or* merchandise.

When your customer fears pressure, and you fear rejection, the result is "retail paralysis."

When your customer judges you, and you judge your customer, nothing happens.

 **To initiate success, initiate "success-behavior."**

Your customers can initiate "success-behavior" by making eye contact, smiling at you, or by asking you for help. But, don't wait for it. It may never happen.

Take control: begin the "trust sale," and start the flow of information. Overcome any fear of rejection by putting aside any first judgment of your customers.

Some customers will act as if they don't *want* to talk to you. Maybe they really *don't* want to talk to you, but they may *need* to. Initiate conversation! The system that follows will show you how.

The system will control your behavior. The system will overcome your feelings and judgments.

You can trust a system that habitualizes "success-behavior." Your behavior will bring about your success. **It's easy.**

Chapter 3

Selling Systematically

The system will work for you, even when you don't feel like working for yourself.

Professionals do their job even when they don't feel like it. Professional athletes do. Secretaries, carpenters, actors, musicians and all kinds of professionals do.

Salespeople are professionals too. Every customer deserves the highest level of service possible, regardless of your mood. Professionalism will make your **success easy**.

Every customer deserves, and should get, your best approach.

 **Decide what your behavior will be *before* your customer walks into the store.**

System: "*A definite scheme or method of procedure.*"

WEBSTER

A successful system eliminates the stress created by poor decision making. It allows you to learn the proper method.

For instance, Las Vegas casinos use a *system* that allows the dealers to win for them. The dealers aren't professional gamblers, yet they consistently win for the casino.

Everyone goes to Las Vegas *hoping to win;* the casino *will win.* The difference is a *system.* We let our feelings and judgments determine our behavior. The casino uses a system. All dealers must follow that system or lose their jobs.

Amateur gamblers react to their feelings and lose their money. They stress, sweat and worry while the dealer remains calm and cool. The gambler doesn't know what to do. The dealer doesn't have to decide what to do; the system dictates it. **It's easy.**

Most people have played blackjack or 21. The game is simple. Everyone gets two cards and has the option of taking more. The goal is to get as close to 21 as possible without going over it. You look at your two cards and think: "Should I or shouldn't I take another card?"

You feel stress anytime you are faced with "Should I or shouldn't I?" Stress binds you and blinds you. Your judgment and feelings control your decisions.

In blackjack, the dealers give you an apparent advantage. They show you one of their cards, but you don't have to reveal either of yours. You also have the advantage of watching fellow gamblers take another card.

You count the cards, and calculate the odds. Your feelings control your decision. You *feel* lucky. You follow your hunches.

Let's see: you have a 10 and a seven, that's 17, and all you need is a four to get 21. A three gets you 20, a two makes 19 and an ace 18.

You look at the dealer's face-up card and see it's a 10. You make a decision. You don't know what the dealer's hidden card is, but you know it might be something larger than your seven.

If the dealer has an eight, nine or 10 hidden, it will beat your 17. You think: "Should I or shouldn't I?" Your feelings tell you to take another card. You say, "Hit me," and they do.

The house wins. It doesn't have to win every hand because it wins every day. If the casino won every hand, no one would play. It wins every day because the dealers are trained to follow a system that is designed to win.

The dealers' behavior is not determined by feelings or judgment. The dealers' behavior is predetermined and institutionalized. **It makes success easy**.

Experienced gamblers go into a room away from the *emotion* of gambling, and calculate the odds. They calculate in advance that in the long run it will not pay to take another card when you have 17 or more. The casino doesn't allow its dealers to make that mistake.

The dealers *must* "stand" on 17 regardless of the other cards showing on the table. In fact, they *tell you* their system, and they *still win*. A sign on the table reads: "Dealer must stand on 17."

Players think that gives them an advantage. They can take another card and the dealer can't. They can use *judgment* the dealer can't. It's their own *judgment* that defeats them. The dealers' *system* assures the casino's victory.

Don't make the mistake of making decisions in the "heat of battle." If you wait until your customer walks into your store, and allow your judgment and feelings to influence your behavior, you will lose and so will your customer. Your feelings change from day to day; your performance shouldn't.

Some days you *feel good* and it's easy to do well. On days that you feel sick or tired it's more difficult to do things right. Your customer should not have to bear the brunt of your feelings.

Your judgment might fail you too. If you let what you *think* about your customer determine how you *act,* then you may not act at all.

Athletes put on their "game face."
Gamblers put on their "poker face."
Customers put on their "shopping face."

If you let that "face" affect your behavior, you might ignore your customer and you'll both lose.

When you follow a system that is designed to win, you *will* win. **It's easy**. You won't make *every* sale, but you will make *more* sales, *every day*.

In gambling, there is always a winner *and* a loser. In selling, there are *only* winners *or* losers. Salespeople who follow a winning system allow their customers and themselves to win. The winning customer gets the needed information, and buys the product. The salesperson makes the sale. It's a **"win/win"** relationship.

Remember, your customer has more to gain from the purchase than you do, regardless of the cost of the product or how large your commission is. The product will last your customer longer than the money will last you or your store.

There may be a big commission in selling a Rolls Royce, but the buyer will be driving and enjoying the car long after the salesperson and car dealer have spent their commissions.

Do your job *for* your customer. Your job is to *give* sufficient information so your customer can make an intelligent buying decision, be it *yes* or *no*.

Start by greeting *all* customers in a sincere and friendly manner, whether they have on their "shopping face" or not.

Do your job whether you feel good or not. Institutionalize success... **it's easy**.

Successful selling happens in three stages and should occur in this order:

    1. Establish communication.
    2. Give information.
    3. Assist in the buying decision.

A rocket ship reaches orbit in three stages which must occur in this order:

1. Establish lift-off.
2. Exit the earth's atmosphere.
3. Enter orbit.

If you watch a rocket ship, you will notice the most powerful engines are responsible for lift-off. Once lift-off is achieved, the first stage is jettisoned, and the next set of smaller engines take the rocket beyond the earth's atmosphere.

Once in orbit, the smallest engines control the rocket ship's direction. Yet if these smallest engines were fired to achieve lift-off, the mission would fizzle.

Likewise, salespeople who attempt to sell merchandise without establishing communication and providing information will fail. You must progress through each of the three stages to make **retail selling easy**.

Establishing communication is like overcoming gravity. You must erase the "shopping face" and relax your customers.

If you saw a friend's car stopped at a red light and you wanted to speak to him or her, you would knock on the window and wait for it to come down before talking.

 **Customers walk into stores with their "windows" up. Get the "windows" down, and establish communication.**

I was retained by a major Waikiki hotel to improve sales in its retail stores. To prepare for my first meeting with the store owners and employees, I went shopping in the hotel as a "mystery shopper."

As part of my research, I walked into a beautiful jewelry store. I observed a professional-looking female employee sitting behind the counter. She looked up at me expressionless, said nothing, then looked back down.

I put on my "shopping face" and began browsing. I peered into the sparkling showcases and saw a huge inventory of very expensive jewelry.

Out of the corner of my eye I saw the saleswoman silently checking me out. I was not sure if she was waiting for an opportunity to speak, or just making sure I wasn't stealing.

I "cruised" the store for five or six minutes in total silence. Is that a long time to be ignored? It sure is. Try holding your breath for that long.

As I left the store, the saleswoman's dull voice hit me in the back of my head. She said, "Are you sure you don't want to buy a gift or something?" I turned around and answered, "No, thank you. I was just looking." She looked away, and I walked away.

Consider the three stages of a sale. She started at stage three. She attempted to assist me in my buying decision without establishing communication or giving me any information.

Perhaps it was my fault; I had my "shopping face" on. If I had been friendlier and asked some questions, she might have done a better job. Instead, she fizzled.

I left the store wondering where she learned her misguided approach. Did she really *expect* her system to work, or was she just seeking permission to go back to sleep? I suspect the latter.

If she knew her approach would fail, why did she say anything at all? Why didn't she just let me leave the store as quietly as I had entered? The probable answer can be summed up in one word: guilt. She wanted to feel as though she had tried.

The owner might call the store later and ask how sales are. She wants to tell the truth. She can say, "It's slow." If the owner asks, "Are people are coming into the store?", she can say, "Yes, but they are just looking." If asked if she had talked to them, she can say, "Yes." It's the truth.

If all store owners watched a video tape of what every customer experiences in their store, any of three statistics might rise dramatically: murder, suicide, or unemployment.

Another time I walked into an art gallery with a similar mission. Here I encountered a totally different approach. The salesperson bounced up from behind his desk and said, "Hi, come on in; we've got the most beautiful art on the island." Without pausing, he continued: "Look at this painting over here."

He walked across the gallery, pointing and saying, "This artist uses the latest technique of electronic laser painting. He uses electrodes to brighten the colors by adjusting the voltage. Notice how bright the painting is over there and how dim it is over here — blah... blah... blah..."

When he finally took a breath, I said, "Yes, it is very nice, but I'm looking for my girlfriend. I'll be back later."

He attempted to corral me, but I broke free and escaped his verbal grasp. He looked frustrated as I left. He knew I wouldn't be back. So did I.

If he had known what I was thinking while he was telling me about the laser painting, he would have changed his approach.

I was thinking two things:
1. "That's the ugliest piece of art I've seen in a long time."
2. "How can I get out of here without being rude?"

His non-stop monologue allowed me to plan my exit. Once he took a breath, I was gone. He offered good information without first establishing communication.

I never saw all of the art in the gallery. I might have seen something I liked if he had given me the opportunity.

> *People don't care how much you know*
> *until they know how much you care.*

 **Communication must be two-way. Establish a dialogue with your customers, not a monologue.**

Pro-Active No-Pressure Selling

The next nine chapters of this book present a nine-step selling system that will show you how to successfully establish communication, give information, and assist in the buying decision.

The system is called "Pro-Active, No-Pressure Selling." You must be pro-active and at the same time remember that no one likes to be pressured. To be "pro-active," yet "no-pressure," is a science.

It's easy to find inactive or reactive no-pressure selling. That's what I found in the jewelry store. It's also common to find pro-active, high-pressure selling. That's what I experienced in the art gallery.

Pro-active people initiate action. People in elevators stare down at their keys or watch the floor numbers flash by. They are *inactive*. Someone who says, "Hello" is being *pro-active*. People who return the "Hello" are *reactive*.

At all times, you are either pro-active, inactive or reactive.

 **The pro-active salesperson makes the most sales.**

People go to nightclubs to dance. Pro-active people ask others to dance. Reactive people accept or reject the pro-active ones. The inactive people lean against the wall and pretend they don't want to dance. They are "just looking."

Who gets the most dances? The pro-active people. They are not always the best looking, or the best dancers. They just dance the most. Who gets the most rejections? You got it: the same people.

Pro-active salespeople get the most sales, and also the most rejections. Rejection can be painful, and sometimes turns pro-activity into inactivity.

When you ask someone to dance and are refused, you must take the "long walk" back to your table. It hurts. You can avoid that pain by not asking anyone else to dance.

No one will walk up to the inactive person and say, "Excuse me, I don't want to dance with you." You trigger the rejection by being pro-active.

A customer will not approach an inactive salesperson and say, "Excuse me, I am just looking." The pro-active salesperson hears it often.

Pro-active, *high pressure* people keep talking when rejected. They increase the pressure and lose the sale.

In the dance club, pro-active, *high pressure* people ask, "Would you like to dance?" When rejected, they might say, "Aw, come on, why not? You're dancing with other people, what's wrong with me?" They won't get a second chance.

Pro-active, *no-pressure* people also ask, "Would you like to dance?" When rejected, they take the pressure off by saying, "Okay, relax and have a good time. I'll check with you later." They back-off. They keep the door open for a re-engagement. They re-engage later. They dance.

 **The key to pro-active, no-pressure selling, (or dancing) is sensitivity.**

When pro-active, *no-pressure* salespeople greet customers with, "Hello," and are told, "I'm just looking," or receive a cold response, they are sensitive. They back off, and they take the pressure off. They relax their customers so they can re-approach later. They keep the door open. They re-approach later. They make the sale.

The nine-step system that follows teaches you how to behave in a *pro-active, no-pressure* manner. Remain pro-active through each of the nine steps. Remain sensitive. Keep the pressure off.

Re-approach. Realize that "no" doesn't always mean "no;" sometimes it means "No, not yet."

Pro-Active, No-Pressure Selling
Nine Steps to Success

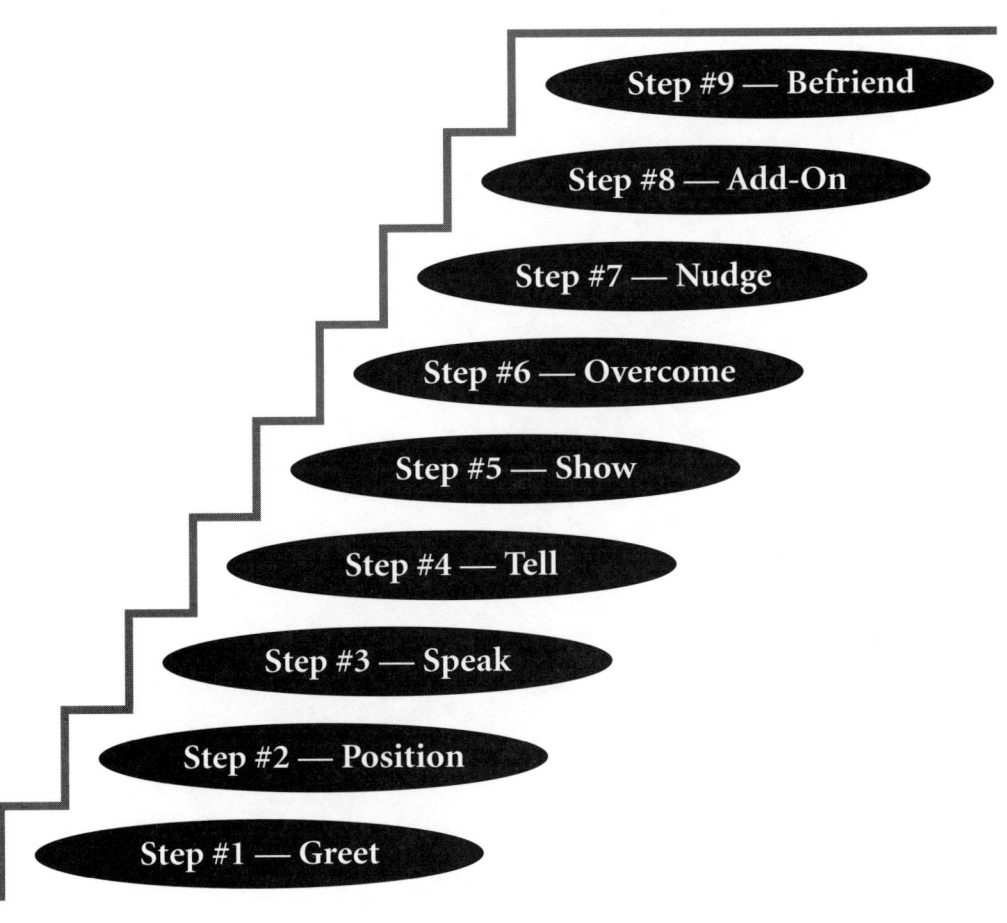

Chapter 4

Selling Yourself

*You get only one chance to make
a first impression.*

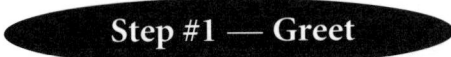

Step #1 — Greet

First impressions are lasting impressions, especially in retail selling. A sale is often made or lost in the first seven seconds. You must make the "trust sale" before you can make the merchandise sale.

Many customers walk into a store looking for the salespeople first: not because they are anxious to talk to them, but they want to identify them, and size up any possible threat.

There are three basic types of customers:
1. Customers who know they *are* going to buy.
2. Customers who know they are *not* going to buy.
3. Customers who are *not sure if* they are going to buy.

The "for sure" buyers will ask for your help. They will demand service. They call out, "Can I get some help over here?"

The "not sure" customers may try to avoid you. Ironically, they need your help the most.

 **Think 20/20/60: 20% of your customers will buy regardless of what you say or do, 20% won't buy regardless of what you say or do, and 60% will buy or not buy depending *totally* upon what you say *and* do.**

Pro-Active, No-Pressure Selling is designed to sell to the 60%. *Anybody* can sell to the first 20%, and *nobody* can sell to the second 20%. Proper behavior with the 60% ensures your success.

Proper behavior begins with making the best possible first impression. You influence each customer's first impression by:

1. How you *look*.
2. How you *act*.
3. What you *say*.

To make the best first impression, *look* professional, *act* alert and enthusiastic, and *say* the right words. **It's easy**.

How you look:
Your looks are a combination of your dress and grooming. What you sell dictates how you should dress.

Someone selling T-shirts might get away with wearing a T-shirt. Anyone selling art or jewelry should never wear a T-shirt.

Many companies provide uniforms to control the appearance of their employees. Others have dress codes or guidelines. A store with more than one employee visible should consider some form of uniform or dress code. It identifies the salespeople, communicates trust and credibility, and controls first impressions.

Many salespeople resist uniforms at first but ultimately learn to like them. They eventually say: "It's great. I don't have to worry about what to wear to work." The uniform becomes part of the system. *Systems* replace judgment and feelings. **Systems make success easy.**

The basic rules of dress are: Don't *overdress* or *underdress*. Dressing is part of the system. Always add two ingredients to the system:

1. Your personality.
2. Common sense.

Common sense says that a salesperson selling clothes in a posh boutique on Rodeo Drive in Beverly Hills will dress up more elegantly than someone selling children's clothing in a mall.

 **Overdressing competes with, and intimidates, your customer. Underdressing communicates a lack of professionalism or pride in your job.**

Grooming is as important as dress. Store owners and salespeople should pay careful attention to grooming. Grooming includes smelling fresh, looking neat and being clean. Attention to clothes, hygiene, fingernails, shoes and hair is essential.

I met a salesperson on an airplane recently. I was impressed with his appearance and demeanor. He was moving to Hawaii and seeking a retail sales position. He had good credentials, and I felt inclined to recommend him to one of my many clients who is always looking for good salespeople.

Everything looked promising until he handed me his business card and I saw a well-packed ring of dirt under his thumbnail. That did it! I put his card in my pocket until I found a trash can to throw it in.

I could be accused of harsh judgment, but customers act the same way. *First impressions are lasting impressions.*

It only takes a minute to review your appearance before going to the sales floor. A small piece of spinach or pepper between your teeth can kill a big sale. Your customers won't tell you what turned them off. This well-qualified person on the airplane never found out why I didn't call him.

Even uniforms require good personal grooming habits. A clean, pressed uniform looks much better than a slightly soiled or wrinkled one.

Think head-to-toe when you look in the mirror. You can destroy a great appearance by wearing a scruffy pair of worn shoes.

How You Act:

You make the best first impression when you are focused and busy. When approaching customers, stand upright, look them in the eye, and smile before speaking.

Avoid putting your hands in your pockets or behind your back. Keep them comfortably at your side.

A well-dressed, well-groomed salesperson standing in the doorway with folded arms will keep customers out of the store. A salesperson leaning against the wall, eyeing the door, might cause customers to make an abrupt U-turn out the door.

Two or more salespeople chit-chatting behind the counter will surely turn-off customers. "You only get one chance to make a first impression."

Salespeople who read, eat or talk to friends on the telephone also make negative first impressions.

 **Customers see you before you see them.**

What You Say:

A sharp-looking, poised salesperson can ruin everything with the wrong first words. Your first 10 words are more important than your next 10,000 words. If your first ten words threaten or turn off your customers, they will not hear anything else.

Your first words should be relaxing and interesting. They should capture your customer's attention. Take advantage of your only chance to make a first impression.

Two approaches to avoid are:
   1. Attack
   2. Ignore

Some salespeople come on too strong; others *ignore* customers to *avoid* attacking them. One is just as bad as the other.

A friendly, sincere greeting at the door is not an attack. A robotic, impersonal greeting is barely better than none at all.

Formal store greetings started when Sam Walton opened his first Wal-Mart store. Sam was thankful that customers traveled long distances to shop at his Wal- Mart. He was *so* grateful that he personally greeted them at the door, welcomed them to his store, helped them to their car and thanked them when they left.

The heart of Sam Walton still beats in his employees today, long after his death. When you enter a Wal-Mart or Sam's Club you *will* be greeted.

It's no accident or coincidence that Wal-Mart's sales have surpassed others in the discount retail industry. He was not the first discount retailer to come along... he *was* the first to institutionalize the greeting process.

Wal-Mart's success was soon imitated, but not always understood. Now we see greeters at K-Mart, This Mart and That Mart. There is a difference. Too many times, the greeting is given by someone who doesn't *want* to greet people, but has been told to do so. It shows.

Another retailer to formalize the greeting process was the Disney Store. Walt Disney would be proud of the way his "retail characters" welcome customers into the Disney Store.

Everyone at Disney follows an important rule. They are never seen "out of character." This is true at theme parks and retail stores alike. Everyone plays a role, and it's *always* remembered.

If you saw Mickey Mouse smoking a cigarette, it would surely break the magic. If you went into the restroom and saw Goofy's feet in the stall next to you, you would be disenchanted.

Disneyland has secret tunnels where "characters" can take breaks, eat and use the restrooms. They remain "in character" whenever visible to customers. They keep the magic working.

Enter the door of a Disney Store, and a "character" greets you. It won't be Mickey Mouse or Donald Duck. It will be a real person playing a *role* . The *role* is a friendly, sincere greeter.

Shortly after Disney's retail success, Warner Brothers began opening retail stores. I visited the Honolulu store soon after it opened. A door greeter slipped in and out of character as customers entered and departed the store.

The greeter leaned against the doorjamb looking tired and bored until a customer approached the door. Then she "came alive" and said, "Welcome to Warner Brothers." When the customer was out of sight, she went "back to sleep."

Do not turn the magic on and off. Remember: customers *see you before you see them.* Warner Brothers would be better off building a mechanical Bugs Bunny than employing a mechanical human being.

The **"SIX KEYS"** to a *sincere, effective* retail greeting are:

- **Eye Contact**
- **Smile**
- **Speak Up**
- **Shut Up**
- **Observe**
- **Mirror**

Memorize the order of these "six keys." Understand how and why they work. Use them and you will make a positive first impression at the door or anywhere in your store. Your sales will increase.

Eye Contact

Eye contact should be *pupil-to-pupil,* not eye-to-eye, eye-to-face or eye-to-body. Every individual is different; look every customer in the eye.

 **The eye is the window to the soul. Make a soul-to-soul connection when you greet someone.**

See a bull's-eye when you make eye contact. People trust someone who "can look them in the eye." You must make the "trust sale" before you can make the merchandise sale.

When you make a pupil-to-pupil connection, you will remember the people you greet. You will recognize them the next time you see them.

2. Smile

Never give customers that "stretched lip smile" you give strangers. Show teeth. Smiling people are more approachable.

Let's say you were at a dance club deciding who you wanted to dance with. Someone who looked directly at you and smiled would be *easy* to ask.

Many customers have a question on their mind, but never ask it. When they meet a smiling employee who looks them in the eye, **it's easy**: they ask it.

3. Speak Up

The pro-active person talks first. You get lucky when your customer is pro-active. Most customers are reactive or inactive. You must be pro-active.

As you make eye contact and smile, simply say, "Hello."

Other appropriate greetings are: "Hi," "Good Morning," "Good Afternoon," "Good Evening," and in Hawaii we say, "Aloha."

🔑 4 — Shut up

The hardest thing to teach salespeople is to shut up. Many salespeople think they must talk to appear smart.

> *"It's better to be quiet and thought of as a fool than to open your mouth and remove all doubt."*

Remember that you are being judged by your customers. Anything you say after your greeting detracts from it. *Anything you say may be held against you.*

"Hello" is a greeting; "Hello, may I help you?" is a threatening question that's used too much. The equally common response is: "No, thank you. I'm just looking."

Another well-used opener is: "Hi, how are you today?" The usual response is: "Fine." The less you give the customer to judge you by in this initial greeting, the better.

Less is more. Just say, "Hello," then shut up. **It's easy.**

🔑 5 — Observe

Study your customer's response to your greeting. You will greet two types of customers:

    1. Those who *want* to talk to you.

    2. Those who *don't want* to talk to you.

Sensitive salespeople recognize who's who. *Both* are good customers. Sensitive salespeople continue talking to the open-minded customers, and give space to the closed-minded or suspicious ones.

Your customer's response to your "hello" may be subtle. Observe it. The customer who wants to talk to you will act differently from the one who doesn't. Be sensitive. Shut up and observe.

 **Your customer's *response* to what you say is more important than *what* you say.**

Your first 10 words are more important than your next 10,000. Measure their effect. Shut up, observe and mirror. **It's easy.**

Mirror

When you observe your customers' reaction to your greeting, act as they do. If they smile back at you and return your greeting, continue smiling and say, "Welcome."

If they give you the stretched lip smile, ignore you, or attempt to escape, make it easy for them to do so. When they move away from you, *step back*. Take the pressure off. *Step back* and disengage, but remain mentally connected. Continue to observe and mirror.

When customers are ready for your help, their body language will change. They look for you.

The sensitive salesperson recognizes this subtle change, re-engages, and moves ahead. Insensitive salespeople prejudge their customer's cool response as a lack of interest. They go on to another task, and miss the subtle signal to re-engage.

Timing is everything. Make eye contact, smile and say, "Hi." If your customer says, "I'm just looking," say, "Take your time; look around." Shut up and back off, but remain mentally connected. Your time will come.

Chapter 5

Selling Silently

Actions speak louder than words.

Step #2 — Position

When selling, you are always:
1. With a customer.
2. Without a customer.

 **There is nothing more threatening to a customer than a salesperson without a customer, unless it's two or three salespeople without a customer.**

Every retailer has experienced the "feast or famine" phenomenon. Being without a customer can seem like forever. However, when one customer comes in the store others will follow. There are definite reasons for this.

Salespeople without customers can unknowingly keep customers out of the store with their physical positioning.

Potential customers walk by the store, look in, see the "available" salesperson, and keep walking. They avoid the possibility of being attacked. They do not want the full attention of a hungry salesperson.

The empty store might also say something about the product or service. There is an old adage about not eating in an empty restaurant.

The busy store attracts customers. The busy salesperson attracts the first customer. When customers look into a store full of people they know it's safe to enter. They know they will not receive the undivided attention of a hungry salesperson.

It's **red light — green light**. Keep the green light on by keeping the red light off.

Red light

The red light is on when the salesperson is clearly visible, and unoccupied.

I walked into one of my stores one day and was told, "It's really slow today; nobody is coming into the store." Yet I noticed ample traffic on the sidewalk outside. I asked the salesperson to come outside and help me identify the problem.

We walked across the street and watched people as they walked by and looked in the store. In a few minutes a customer entered the store, then another, then another.

My salesperson was eager to run across the street and start selling. But I held her back saying, "Just wait and watch. We came out here to analyze our problem and we seem to have solved it." What was our problem?

When I removed my salesperson, I solved the problem, but obviously created another one. Now there was no one in the store to sell.

If I had turned my salesperson loose to charge into the store, she would have run the customers out.

 **A charging bull will stampede the grazing cattle.**

Imagine a traffic light over your store door. The green light says, "Come on in." The red light says, "Stay out." My salesperson had the red light on.

By effectively removing the threat, we turned the green light on. The first customer to enter the store saw an empty store without a salesperson, and *cautiously* entered. The next customer saw a customer without a salesperson, and *willingly* entered.

The others saw a crowd — they *eagerly* entered.

You have to keep the green light on *and* stay in the store.

Here are a few red light positions to avoid:

Salesperson blocking the door — This is the surest way to keep customers out of your store. A salesperson standing in the doorway, blocking the entrance while waiting for customers, might wait forever.

🚦 **Salesperson just outside the door** — Have you ever seen a salesperson taking a smoke or coffee break on the sidewalk outside a store? It's a turn-off. Customers see you before you see them. They keep walking.

🚦 **Salesperson behind the counter** — Only employees go behind counters. An idle salesperson standing or sitting behind the counter is a threat. It keeps customers out of the store.

🚦 **Two or more salespeople talking with each other** — "Vulture Gulch." Two or three against one – "No, thank you!"

🚦 **Salesperson on the phone, eating, or visiting with friends** — This creates a compounding negative first impression, and a negative second impression if and when the salesperson switches his or her focus to the customer.

Here's how to get the green light on:

🚦 **Green Light**

The green light comes on automatically when you are busy with a customer. You must *consciously* switch it on when you are not with a customer. You do so by getting busy. **To get busy, be busy. It's easy.**

Most retail salespeople have other duties besides selling. They stock shelves, tag merchandise, clean glass, take inventory, vacuum the floor, answer the phone, and so on.

Do these tasks in such a manner as to create motion and attract customers. Once a customer enters your store, stop doing the other task and greet your customer.

Let's analyze a few green light positions:

Salesperson doing paperwork — Whenever possible, do your paperwork from the *customer side* of the counter. Customers are more likely to enter the store if they are not *sure* you work there.

Customers might think you are a vendor, or a customer filling out a form. Don't go behind counters when you are alone in the store. Keep the green light on. **It's easy.**

Stocking shelves — Look as focused as possible when stocking, folding or counting merchandise.

Position yourself with your back to the door and use the "eyes in the back of your head" to watch for customers. When customers enter the store, let them take several steps into the store, then look up and greet them.

Using the telephone — First rule: avoid personal telephone calls. When business requires you to talk on the telephone, try to do so from the customer side of the counter.

When talking on the phone always stand erect, and be alert to customers entering your store. When you see customers in your store, get off the phone as soon as possible, and greet them.

Act like you are a customer — When you find yourself with nothing to do, and no customers are in the store, become one. Act like a customer who is alone in the store — it's a real attraction.

Put your hands behind your back and "just look". Touch or hold up the merchandise for a closer look.

This can be time well spent. Rehearse "information giving" in your mind. Pick up an item and say to yourself: "How would I describe this to a customer?"

When a customer enters the store, put the item down and greet the customer.

Role play — As mentioned earlier, two or more salespeople without customers can be the biggest threat of all. Working with another salesperson gives you the opportunity to practice your techniques on each other. Practice makes perfect.

Practice your greeting, practice backing off, practice giving information, practice being pro-active. Team up for success.

When a customer enters the store, stop practicing and greet the customer.

Position yourself properly, control traffic flow and make success easy.

After greeting your customer, continue to monitor your "positioning" and notice how your customer is responding to it. Be *sensitive*.

When you re-approach, be aware of:
1. Which side you approach from.
2. How close you get to your customer.

When deciding which side to approach from, remember that you represent a potential threat. You have not completed the "trust sale" yet, and your approach might push your customer away from you.

 **Ask yourself: "Which direction would I prefer my customer to move?" Then, approach from the opposite side.**

If you prefer your customer move to the left, approach from the right, and vice versa.

The general rule is to position yourself between your customer and the door. It's not your intention to scare or move your customers away from you, but if you do, you would rather scare them *into the store* than *out the door.*

Always give your customers an escape route away from you and further into your store. This is very subtle, and yet very important.

Keeping your customer in your store is an essential part of **making retail selling easy**.

How close can you get to your customer? The answer is: "It depends on the customer." Everyone is different. People need varying amounts of "space" to be comfortable.

Picture an invisible "bubble" around all customers. It represents the area you are not allowed to enter.

If you invade someone's personal space, he or she will move away from you. If your customer requires two feet of space to be comfortable, and you come within one foot, your customer will move one foot away from you. It's easier than pushing you back.

Insensitive salespeople "push" customers around the store by "hovering" too close until they finally escape by leaving the store. They are not given the opportunity to relax and look closely at anything.

Approaching a customer is being pro-active. Remain **sensitive,** and you will know when you have gotten too close. When you get too close, *step back* and take the pressure off.

 **You sometimes need to get *too close* in order to find out *how close* you *can get.***

Your customers will tell you with their body language when you get too close. They will turn and look the other way, stiffen slightly, stand upright or walk away.

Approach slowly, be sensitive, step back and remain pro-active without pressure. **It's easy**.

Make it inviting for your customers to enter your store; then make it desirable for them to stay. You can do most of this without speaking. *Actions speak louder than words.*

Remain sensitive, give people their space, and your words will be welcomed. You will open the door of communication and lower resistance.

Now you can *speak*.

Chapter 6

Selling Openers

Your first ten words are more important than your next 10,000.

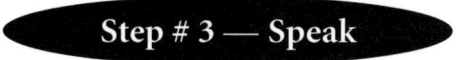

Step # 3 — Speak

Everybody has a mission. You make retail selling easy when you get in sync with your *customer's* mission.

Your customer's mission is not necessarily to buy, nor is it to waste time. Your customer's mission is to *"discover."* It is to *discover* more about your store.

Customers know what *type* of merchandise you sell. They don't know about its quality, quantity, cost or about *you*. They came in to find out.

Customers judge *you* first. You must make the "trust sale" before you can make the merchandise sale.

You make a positive, non-threatening, first impression with your appearance and posture. Now it's time to *speak*.

 **Your first words must tell your customers that you understand their mission.**

First words that figuratively say, "Give me your money," or "Let's waste some time," are common. These words communicate a mission that is different from that of your customer's.

It's time for "lift-off." It's time to "overcome gravity" and establish communication. It's time to establish *meaningful, straightforward* communication.

Your customer came in to *discover* more about your store. Talk about your store first.

 **As you practice the nine steps to Pro-Active, No-Pressure Selling, remember to add two ingredients: personality and common sense.**

If a customer walks into your store and announces, "I'm in a hurry and I want to buy this and that; here's my credit card," forget the nine steps and ring it up. That's common sense.

Common sense also dictates differences when dealing with longtime established customers as compared to customers you have never seen before. It's important that you make that distinction before speaking. Ask yourself, "Have I seen this person in my store before?" The answer to this question dictates your first words.

By using the six keys to a sincere and effective greeting, you will remember whom you have greeted before.

When you make a pupil-to-pupil connection you will remember that person.

Before identifying the *best* first words to use, let's reveal the most commonly used *worst* words. If you are using these words now, it will take some practice to change your habits.

New behavior is *awkward* at first, but when you *apply* it, it becomes *automatic.*

What's best for your customer is best for you.

I go to shopping centers almost every day. I walk in and out of retail stores and analyze the approaches of salespeople.

Sadly, the most common approach is a no-approach. Most salespeople expect their customers to be pro-active. They avoid rejection. They miss success.

Salespeople who *are* pro-active, are mostly in the "attack" mode. The most common retail opening question is, "May I help you?" What's wrong with this question? It sounds harmless, like an offer of help.

Your *job* is to help customers. You don't have to seek permission to do your job. You wouldn't ask, "Is it okay with you if I do my job now?" You shouldn't ask, "May I help you?" You should *just do it.*

When salespeople ask you, "May I help you?" what type of help do you feel they have in mind? The next time a salesperson asks, "May I help you?" say, "Yes, could you get me a cup of coffee while I look around?" or "Yes, would you go out and put a quarter in the parking meter for me?" or "Yes, would you keep an eye on my kids while I shop?"

You know what kind of help these salespeople are offering. They are offering to sell you something. You respond with "No, thank you. I'm just looking."

You don't want your customer to say, "No, thank you. I'm just looking," so don't ask, "May I help you?"

Another common opener many salespeople use is "How are you today?" That's nice, but do your customers believe you really care?

This is a "small talk opener" that leads to more small talk, and moves you away from the sale.

Always open with a non-threatening question. Questions give you control. Questions demand answers. Answers require thought.

It's important that the question is not threatening or negative. "May I help you?" is threatening. "How are you today?" produces an unpredictable and possibly negative response.

The rule when asking questions is: **Never ask a question that *might* get you an answer you *don't* want to hear.**

Your goal is to initiate *meaningful, straightforward* communication. Start on the right foot. Get in sync with your customer's mission. Your customer's mission is to DISCOVER. "May I help you?" implies it is to buy.

"How are you today?" implies the mission is to waste time. Customers are not in your store to waste time and make small talk with you. People *don't* walk by your store, look in and say, "Let's go inside and tell that salesperson how we are doing today."

Your customers come into your store to *discover*. Begin the discovery by being *straightforward;* your customers will appreciate it. It will make your **success easy.**

When greeting a customer ask yourself, "Have I seen this person in my store before?" Your answer will be "Yes," or "No." Your answer then determines your opening question.

The customer's reaction to your initial greeting dictates when you ask the opening question. Timing is everything. After you say "Hello," shut up, observe and mirror. The mirror tells you when to speak next. If your customer "opens up" immediately, you can proceed directly to the opening question.

If your customer walks away, you should back off, remain mentally connected, maintain the proper position, and wait for the right moment to re-engage and ask the opening question. **It's easy.**

Your best opening questions are:

1. "Nice to see you again. When were you in last?"
2. "Have you been in our store before?" or
"Is this your first time in our store?"

These are questions that will get you the answers you *want* to hear. These are non-threatening, *straightforward* questions that put you in sync with your customer's mission.

These questions begin the *discovery* process and open the door for you to give meaningful information. These are questions that have predictable responses that give you control. These are questions that **make retail selling easy**.

Customers You Recognize

Question: "Nice to see you again. When were you in last?"
Response: "Yesterday", or "Last week." (recently)
Question: "What brought you back?"

If your customer was in your store recently something created the return. Find out what it is.

Question: "Nice to see you again. When were you in last?"
Response: "Last year", or "A few months ago." (not so recently)
Statement: "Welcome back. We have made a few changes since then ..." (proceed to step #4 — next chapter)

When you recognize customers and determine it has been awhile since they have been in the store, they are on a *rediscovery mission*. Get in sync. Tell them what's new, what's on sale, what's been relocated.

Customers You Don't Recognize

Question: "Have you been in our store before?"
Response: "Yes."
Question: "Welcome back. When were you in last?"

You have *now* discovered that this customer *has* been in your store before. Follow the system as previously explained.

Question: "Have you been in the store before?"
Response: "No"
Statement: "Welcome." (Proceed to step #4-next chapter)

Step #3 — SPEAK, *sets you up* to talk about your store. It launches the discovery mission. It makes a sincere first impression. It *sets you up* to move to step #4, and *tell* your customer about your store.

Chapter 7

Selling The Discovery

Discovery... "To make known or visible..." WEBSTER

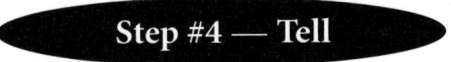

Step #4 — Tell

If you gave this eight-question quiz to every customer leaving your store, how many would pass?

1. What is the name of our store?
2. How long have we been in business?
3. How many locations do we have, and where are they?
4. What is our theme?
5. What do we sell?
6. Where is our merchandise located?
7. What's on sale?
8. What's new?

If your customers knew the answers to these eight questions, they would enjoy their shopping experience, and the store would be more profitable.

 **The more your customers know about your store and where things are, the easier their shopping experience is.**

Customers who have to search for what they want sometimes never find it. They leave the store without it. Don't make your customers look at *everything* to find the *right thing*.

 **People looking at everything, see nothing.**

Customers looking at everything get into a rejective state of mind. They think, "I *don't* need that; I *don't* want these; this is *not* what I'm looking for." Before they know it, they walk right past what they *are* looking for.

Do you know the answers to the eight-question quiz about your own store? It's amazing how many store employees don't know all of the answers.

To practice this discovery step you must first know the information yourself, then script it in your mind.

Be prepared to tell the *whole* story to an interested customer. Be prepared to cut the story *short* to an uninterested customer. **Be sensitive.**

 **Tell your customers *who* you are, *what* you are, *what* you sell, and *where* it is, in a pro-active, no-pressure manner.**

Remain sensitive as you offer this "verbal tour" of your store. Keep asking yourself, "Does this customer want to know more?" If the answer is "Yes," continue. If the answer is "No," shut up and back off. Remain *sensitive,* and mentally engaged.

To be *sensitive,* speak up, shut up, observe and "mirror" your customers. After each bit of information, pause and allow your customers to respond. Their subtle responses will tell you if it's okay to continue or not.

Take the pressure off and lower resistance by beginning with *general* information. Start the discovery by asking, "Have you been in the store before?" or "When were you in the store last?" Your customer's answer to this question gets you started.

Remember to add common sense by differentiating between first-time shoppers and regular customers. If you're not sure, find out.

Your "verbal tour" should always begin and end with the same statement, regardless of how lengthy the tour is — whether it lasts five seconds or five minutes. Begin with a "relaxing statement" and end with a "releasing statement." They can be the same.

Relaxing statement: "Relax, enjoy yourself, and look around ..."

Releasing statement: "So relax, enjoy yourself, and look around."

Remember the jewelry store experience I related earlier? The salesperson waited until I was leaving the store before she spoke.

Had she practiced the first four steps of Pro-Active, No-Pressure Selling, it would have gone something like this:

Salesperson: "Hello."

Me: "Hello."

Salesperson: "Welcome. Have you been in our store before?"

Me: "No, I haven't."

Salesperson: "Well, relax, enjoy yourself, and look around... (short pause)

"We are XYZ Jewelers of Honolulu." (shut up-observe-mirror)

"We have been in business for 14 years, and have five stores throughout the islands." (shut up-observe-mirror)

"We specialize in fine jewelry for all occasions." (shut up-observe-mirror)

"For example, you'll find gold chains in that far showcase." (pointing and looking in direction of showcase. Shut up-observe-mirror)

"We have diamond rings and pendants over there." (look-point-shut up-observe-mirror)

"We also have a very large selection of pearls in this case, and our fashion jewelry is in that showcase along the wall." (look-point-shut up-observe-mirror)

"So, relax, enjoy yourself and look around. Ask me any questions you have."

(back off-shut up-observe-mirror)

Remain mentally connected.

At each pause ask yourself, "Does my customer want to hear more?" If so, continue. Each pause gives your customer an opportunity to react. If your customer asks you a question, answer it, pause, then continue.

If your customer looks cold or walks away from you at any time, make your releasing statement earlier, shut up and back off, then continue to observe and mirror.

Remember my "attack experience" in the art gallery? The salesperson never stopped talking long enough to take a breath. A pro-active, no-pressure experience would go like this.

Art consultant: "Hello."

Me: "Hello."

Art consultant: "Welcome to the gallery. Have you been in before?"

Me: "No, I haven't."

Art consultant: "Well, relax, enjoy yourself and look around."

"We are XYZ Gallery." (pause)

"We have been in this location for five years." (pause)

"We have another gallery at the Ritz Hotel in California." (pause-continue)

"As you can see we carry a variety of art styles for our varied clientele."
(pause-continue)

"For example, you'll find original oil paintings in that showroom to the rear of the gallery, created by different artists."
(look-point-pause-continue)

"We also have a wide selection of water colors along this wall."
(point-pause-continue)

"Our island artists are featured in that viewing room over there."
(pointing to the room-pause-continue)

"We also have this selection of high-tech laser paintings over here."
(point-pause-continue)

"We have wooden bowls in that far corner, as well as some jewelry in this front showcase. So relax, enjoy yourself and look around. Ask me any questions you have."

Once "released," I would have been free to go to the area that interested me. For instance, I would *not* have gone to see the laser paintings if I didn't like them. The salesperson would *not* have made the mistake of emphasizing information about something I was *not* interested in.

If the salesperson had used this approach, I might have looked at the island art and been open to specific information. He would have been on safe ground to re-engage. He might have made a sale. It could have been **easy.**

As *you* script a "verbal tour" of *your* store consider the value of the following information.

Store Name – You cannot assume that your customers see your sign, know or remember your name. Reinforcing your store name makes it easier for your customers to call you at a later time or recommend you to someone else. It gives you an identity.

The store owner probably gave a lot of thought to the store name. *Give* the store name to your customer.

Time in Business – The longer you have been in business, the longer you might stay in business. If you just opened yesterday, you might close tomorrow. At least that's the assumption your customer makes. History communicates trust and credibility. Make the "trust sale" before you attempt to make the merchandise sale.

Number of Locations – The more locations you have the more trusted you are. When your customers learn about your other locations they may want to shop there too. They may tell their friends who live in that area about your store.

Your Theme – Understanding your theme or concept makes your store more memorable the next time your customer goes shopping. You may not have what all of your customers need, but maybe you have what their friends need. Maybe they will think of you the next time they are shopping for a gift.

What You Sell —When you offer customers a "menu" of your products you save them time. You also allow them to consider your store for future needs. Describe your merchandise in broad categories. It's okay to point out those laser paintings, but it's not okay to try to sell them to someone who has no interest in them.

Where It Is – Explaining your store layout gives customers a "road map" to follow. It allows them to go directly to their area of interest. It saves them time, and lets you know what their interests are.

Had I loved the laser paintings, as I'm sure some people do, I would have walked directly to them. Specific information would have been appreciated.

What's On Sale – Everybody likes a sale. Many stores have sales on selected merchandise. Don't rely on interior signs to identify your sale merchandise. Build it into your "verbal tour."

What's New - New sells! Give shoppers a chance to see and buy your new merchandise before everyone else does.

I cannot overemphasize the importance of being *sensitive* when practicing your "verbal tour." Some customers don't *care* who you are, what you are, what you sell or where it is. Some customers don't want to hear it. That's okay. Don't force-feed this information to customers who don't want it.

I also want to re-emphasize common sense. Don't tell your *regular* customers who you are every time they enter the store. You should, however, tell them what's new, where things have been moved, or what's on sale.

 **The system gives you a plan to follow. Your common sense and sensitivity make it personal and dynamic.**

Following these first four steps of Pro-Active, No-Pressure Selling might require a minute; it might take five minutes. Your customer's reaction determines how much you should say. Learn the five-minute presentation, and the five-second presentation. Be prepared. **It's easy.**

At this point in the system you have not yet attempted to sell any merchandise. You have only made the "trust sale." You have greeted, welcomed, and *relaxed* your customer. You have said *who* you are, *what* you are, *what* you sell and *where* it is.

Now it's time to sell merchandise. *Selling is giving information.* Your information has been *general* up to this point. Now it's time to get *specific*.

Giving specific information in the proper manner makes **retail selling easy.**

Chapter 8

Selling Specifics

Inform: " To communicate knowledge..." WEBSTER

Step #5 — Show

In order to give your customers sufficient information *you* must be knowledgeable. Learn everything there is to know about your merchandise.

The store's buyer is usually the most knowledgeable employee. Why? Because the buyer has already been a customer. Someone has given the buyer sufficient information to make an intelligent buying decision. Your store's buyer has determined that customers will buy your products.

 **The vast knowledge learned by the buyer must be passed on to the salespeople, then to the customers.**

Pro-active customers will ask questions before buying. Salespeople without sufficient information sometimes guess wrong or say, "I don't know." They lose sales.

I suggest retailers create a 3x5 or 5x7 index card system to communicate product knowledge. A product information card is completed for each item in the store and placed alphabetically in a card file or shoe box. A new product information card is completed every time a new product is added to the store inventory. In its simplest form this card contains three elements:

1. What each product is, who manufactured it, what it does, or how to use it.
2. Five features of the product.
3. Five benefits of the product to the customer.

Salespeople can study the product information cards, and refer to them in times of need.

 **Knowledge is power. Knowledge makes retail selling easy.**

Your customer must realize that the satisfaction received from your product is more beneficial than the money spent.

Have you ever seen a customer stop to look at an item, pick it up, focus on the price tag, then drop it like a hot potato? This reaction is called "sticker shock."

When customers are left on their own to discover information, they may *only* discover *the price*. Price is a *small part* of the information needed to make an intelligent buying decision.

The price, all by itself, is more likely to discourage than encourage a purchase. *Prices don't sell; information does.* Prices tell a very limited story about your product.

In Waikiki, some retailers sell three T-shirts for $10. Other retailers sell one T-shirt for $20. Is a T-shirt a T-shirt?

Without sufficient information, the customer might buy the cheaper priced T-shirt and pay more for it later, in the form of dissatisfaction, product wear and tear, shrinkage, color fading, replacement, etc.

The more expensive T-shirt is made of a higher quality fabric. It has reinforced stitching to maintain its shape. It has been pre-washed and pre-shrunk to keep its size. Its construction is tubular, and its printing is a high quality silk-screen.

The $20 T-shirt will look great several years from now. It lasts. The cheap T-shirt soon becomes a car washrag.

Does your customer know this? No! When your customer picks up the $20 T-shirt and looks at it, you should provide this information. As you add information you make the T-shirt more valuable than the $20.

If you allow your customer to judge your T-shirt as too expensive, your entire store becomes overpriced. Your customer drops the T-shirt, leaves the store, never returns, and passes the word about how expensive your store is.

 **Not giving information is costly. It costs the store business, and it costs the customer the opportunity to buy a better quality product.**

On the other hand, your store might have the high quality T-shirt marked down to an "unbelievably great price." Without knowing why it costs so little, your customers might prejudge it as "cheap" and miss out on a great bargain.

Your customers need *you* to give them sufficient information to make intelligent buying decisions. You cannot rely on signs, labels, or hang tags to do *your* communicating.

Here's an example which illustrates my point. During a visit to San Francisco I wanted to buy a new silk shirt. I was excited about having some shopping choices not available in Hawaii.

I walked in and out of several Union Square stores. I was *ignored* in most stores, and *attacked* in others. Some tried to sell me something that I didn't want.

I eventually discovered a huge selection of silk shirts on the basement level of a large discount store. There were rows and rows of silk shirts. I discovered my size rack and began to explore.

I flipped through the shirts until I saw one I liked. It looked great. I wanted it. Then I looked at the price tag and saw $99.99. Yipes! I put it back.

I've paid more than that for a silk shirt, but this was a *discount* store. I thought, "What a rip-off." Then I looked around for a salesperson. Salespeople are hard to find in most discount stores.

I became pro-active. I found a "clerk" who was tagging some merchandise nearby, and asked, "Why is this shirt so expensive?"

She replied, "Well sir, we just marked that shirt down today."

Now, did I have sufficient information to purchase it, or was I further confused?

I remained pro-active and proceeded to find out more. I asked, "How much was it *before* you marked it down?" She flatly replied, "$39.99."

Now I was *really* confused. I held the shirt as far away from me as my arms could stretch so I could get a better look at the price tag.

As the price came into clear focus I saw that it actually read "$9.99," not "$99.99." It wasn't the store's fault that I failed to wear my reading glasses while shopping.

Was I sold now? No! I was ready to drop the shirt again. "It must be defective," I thought. "I've never seen a silk shirt so cheap." I remained pro-active and asked, "Why is it so cheap?"

She politely answered, "We just received a new shipment of silk shirts yesterday and we were told to mark all of these down to $9.99 and clear them out. They'll all be sold this weekend."

Now what do you think I did? I bought **12** silk shirts. Without further information, $99.99 was "too much," and $9.99 was "too little."

 **Prices confuse; information sells.**

Most customers would not have sought out a clerk and asked the right questions. Most customers would have walked away. I almost walked away. If so, I would have gone home with 12 fewer shirts and missed out on a great deal. **"Lose/lose."**

Fortunately it turned out to be a **"win/win."** The store sold me the 12 shirts, and I'm still wearing some of them.

In this example, everybody got *lucky*. Don't depend on luck for your success; create it.

When your customers look at your merchandise, pro-actively give them the information they need. Do not wait for your customers to ask the right questions. Some customers don't know what to ask; some are afraid or embarrassed to ask.

Giving *specific* information is step #5 in the nine-step Pro-Active, No-Pressure Selling System.

Specific information should be given in "bite-size pieces." *Give* customers one piece of information; then shut up and allow them to react.

 **Pro-Active, No-Pressure information giving works. The key to its success is sensitivity; speak up, shut up, observe, and mirror.**

For example, if you were offering candy samples, you would allow your customers to taste the sample and react before offering another piece. You would study their reactions. If they spit it out you wouldn't ask, "Would you like another?"

As you re-engage with your customers to give specific information be aware of your body language. Think about where you are standing.

Keep your back to the door. Don't get too close to your customer. If you do, step back as you talk.

When giving information, stay a step back and a step to the side of your customers. Do not "put yourself in the picture."

 **Your customers should be looking at your merchandise, not at you.**

As you talk, look at the merchandise you are describing, not at your customer. This focuses your customer's eyes on your merchandise, not on you.

The first "bit" of information you give should be the most obvious. If it's a ring, say it's a ring. If it's a T-shirt, say it's a T-shirt.

You can do this without insulting your customer's intelligence by adding one additional piece of information. Say, "That ring you're looking at is 14K gold," or "That T-shirt you're looking at is 100% cotton." Start with the most obvious. Here are two reasons why:

1. To be sure your customers recognize the obvious — some don't.
2. To get immediate agreement.

At any given moment you are either moving towards the sale, or away from the sale.

 **Whenever you say something that gets customer agreement, you move towards the sale.**

Whenever you say something that gets customer disagreement, you move away from the sale.

To assure customer agreement, keep your information *factual*. Few people will argue with *facts*.

Keep your *opinions* to yourself until asked. Sgt. Joe Friday on the classic "Dragnet" TV series said, "Just the facts, ma'am." He didn't want to be confused or influenced by *opinion*.

When you say, "That painting you are looking at is an original oil painting," your customers aren't likely to respond, "No, it isn't." They say something like, "Oh, I see." You move towards the sale.

If you say, "Isn't that beautiful?" your customers might think, "Well, not really." You move away from the sale.

Has a clothing salesperson ever approached you and said, "That would look great on you." You might not agree, and you move away from the purchase. The salesperson failed to make the "trust sale."

To keep yourself moving towards the sale, keep giving *facts* — in bite-size pieces, with sensitivity. *Speak up, shut up, observe* and *mirror*.

Once you pro-actively offer the first piece of obvious, factual information and shut up, your customer feels "silent pressure." The *pressure* starts when you shut up. Your customer feels *pressured* to respond.

 **The *only* pressure you should *ever* put on your customers is *silent* pressure. Silence is golden.**

More sales are lost by a salesperson saying the *wrong words* than sales are made by a salesperson saying the *right words*.

 **Selling is not talking people into buying. Selling is *allowing* people to buy.**

Give one "bit" of factual information, and shut up. Your customer will remove the pressure by making one of five moves:

The Five Customer Moves
1. Buy it.
2. Walk away from it.
3. Ask a question about it.
4. Silently continue looking at it.
5. Make an excuse for not buying it.

Chess players know the value of anticipating their opponent's next move. When you anticipate, you can plan.

Plan your next move in advance. Know exactly what you will do when your customer makes any one of the five "customer moves" above.

The Five Salesperson Counter Moves:

1. The Customer Buys It: When you shut up and your customer says, "I'll take it," the pressure comes off. *Your* move is: ring up the sale and "add-on." **It's easy**.

Suggest other items in the store that will accentuate or complement what is being purchased. Suggest earrings that go with the ring, shorts that go with the T-shirt, etc.

The words "I'll take it" should *start* the sale, not end the sale. Chapter 11 will show you *specifically* how to "add-on" at the register.

2. The Customer Walks Away From It: If your customer walks away after you say, "The T-shirt is 100% cotton," what else can you say? Nothing!

Silence will move your customers away from merchandise they are *not* going to buy. That's positive. It moves them on to something they *may* buy.

When you rattle off non-stop product information you force your customers to listen politely. Your customers plan their exit. Unwelcome words create negative pressure. Let *silence* do the sales job *for you.*

Allow your customers to escape you when they want to. When you offer a "bit" of information and they walk away, remain silent, and step back. Do not follow customers. Customers that are chased, run!

Disengage, stand back, but remain mentally connected. This takes the pressure off and allows your customers to stop and look at other items. When they do, you can re-engage and start the process over again. *Speak up - shut up - observe* and *mirror.*

3. **The Customer Asks A Question:** When you shut up, you give your customer the opportunity to ask a question. Many customers have questions they haven't asked. Your customer can remove the silent pressure by asking a question.

When you are asked a question, answer it, then *shut up, observe* and *mirror.* The silent pressure goes back on your customer to make one of the five moves again.

Just continue to follow the system. **It's easy.**

4. **The Customer Silently Continues To Look At It:** When you shut up, and your customer continues looking at the merchandise, you are moving towards the sale.

The *silent* pressure is on. Your customer wonders: "Should I or shouldn't I?" You wonder, "Will I make this sale, or not?" The *silent* pressure is intensified. Nobody is talking. Silence is golden. *Decisions* are being made.

Remain quiet and continue looking at the merchandise. Wait approximately three *elongated* seconds before speaking again. I call these three *long* seconds, "KABOOMS."

A "KABOOM" is the sound of *your* heartbeat during this deafening silence. You'll hear it; listen for it. Kaboom-Kaboom-Kaboom.

If your customer continues to look at the merchandise for three *long* seconds after you shut up, then provide the next piece of information, *shut up, observe* and *mirror.*

Say:

"That T-shirt is made of 100% cotton."
Kaboom-Kaboom-Kaboom.

"It is available in small, medium and large."
Kaboom-Kaboom-Kaboom.

"It has been pre-washed, so it won't shrink."
Kaboom-Kaboom-Kaboom.

"Notice the heavy stitching around the collar which allows it to keep its shape over the years."
Kaboom-Kaboom-Kaboom.

If at any time your customer walks away, step back, shut up and remain quiet.

If your customer asks a question, answer it and then shut up. Wait three more "Kabooms," then offer the next piece of information.

Continue to follow the system. **It's easy.**

The *last* piece of information offered should be the *price*. Say, "And it's *only* $20." Always emphasize "only" when giving a price.

Now remain quiet for as many "Kabooms" as it takes for your customer to make the next move. The *silent* pressure is on. Keep it on until your customer removes it.

Your customer has gained sufficient information to make an intelligent buying decision. It's time to make it, *yes* or *no*.

The silence will cause your customer to buy it, walk away from it, ask another question, *or* make the fifth "customer move."

5. The Customer Makes An *Excuse* For Not Buying It: When your customer says, "I want to think about it," you must be prepared.

You can't stop and *think about* what *you* should say next; you have to *know* what you will say. You must be prepared for excuses, and be ready to overcome them.

Learning how to overcome excuses is crucial to making **retail selling easy.** It's the next step to Pro-Active, No-Pressure Selling.

Chapter 9

Selling Objections

Objection... "Reason for or a feeling of disapproval..."
                                                    WEBSTER

Step #6 — Overcome

"It's too expensive."
"I want to think about it."
"I want to look around before I buy."
"I'll be back."

Customers give salespeople these typical excuses everyday.

Most salespeople react in one of two ways, and both are wrong.

 **When hearing excuses, most salespeople either "bear down" or "bail out."**

To "bear down" is to disbelieve the excuse, and push for the sale. Salespeople say: "Aw, come on," or "Go ahead and get it," or "You won't beat that price anywhere," or some other form of begging. *Begging* customers to buy products they do not want will not work.

Other salespeople "bail out." They hand their customers a "ticket out the door." They say, "Okay, here is my business card. We are open everyday until 9 p.m.; please ask for me when you return."

 **A customer who has a *good reason* for *not* buying your product, and leaves your store telling you, "I want to think about it," *won't* be back.**

The problem with "bearing down" or "bailing out" is that you haven't discovered the true objection. Discovering *true* objections leads to sales. It separates the real "salespeople" from the "order takers." It leads to success. **It's easy.**

Buyers are liars. Buyers lie to avoid or eliminate pressure. They lie to protect the salesperson from embarrassment. It's tempting to buy the lie.

If you buy the lie you lose the sale, and you lose your customer, too. A customer who doesn't want your product and tells you, "I'll be back," might avoid you and your store in the future.

Don't buy the lie.

Have you ever been invited to a party you didn't want to attend? Have you ever awakened not wanting to go to school or work? Have you ever been late for an appointment? Have you ever looked at something you didn't want to buy? *Have you ever told a lie?* Have you ever made up an excuse that wasn't totally true?

People with hangovers call in sick. People who don't want to go to a friend's party say, "Something came up." People who oversleep say, "I got stuck in traffic."

People who don't want to buy your merchandise say, "I'll think about it." **Think about it!** *Buyers are liars.*

The truth is not always easy to admit. It's hard to tell your friend that you don't want to go to her party because you don't like her husband. It's tough to tell your boss, "I have a hangover." It's embarrassing to say, "I overslept."

Telling the salesperson "I'll think about it" creates an *easy escape.*

 **You can *overcome* most objections once you know the *truth*.**

To discover the truth, you must accept that it's "okay" for your customers not to buy your merchandise.

Just because a customer spends time with you does not entitle you to the sale. Selling is not talking people into buying. Selling is giving the customer sufficient information to make an intelligent buying decision, *yes* or *no*. *No* is okay if *yes* isn't.

Overcoming objections is a matter of learning something I call your "okay, buts."

 **An "okay, but..." is a planned, rehearsed response to an *anticipated* objection.**

You can anticipate specific objections to your business or products. You should know what they are, then plan and rehearse your "okay, but..." responses.

When people lie, they feel pressure. Your customers know when they are lying, but they don't know how you will respond.

Some customers know they are *not* going to buy your product when they say, "I want to think about it."

When you say "Okay," these customers think they got away with the lie, and relax. The pressure comes off. When you say, "But..." your customers open up and listen.

Now you can now search for the truth.

The Truth is:
1. "I don't like it."
2. "I don't have the money."
3. "I like it, and have the money, but I am not yet convinced it's *okay* to buy it."

Once you know the *true* objection you *can* overcome it. When your customer tells you, "I don't like that color," you know what to do. You find the right color.

When your customer says, "I don't have the money," you suggest something less expensive, or a layaway, or a financing plan. You solve the problem.

If your customer said, "I really want it, and I can afford it. I just need a little reassurance," you *would* offer that reassurance. You *would* make the sale. **It *would* be easy.**

When your customer says, **"I want to think about it,"** say something like, "Okay, but I've found that when someone needs to *think about it*, maybe it's not the *perfect* one. What *might not* be *perfect* with this one?"

Shut up, observe and *mirror*. The "okay, but" phrase makes a pressure relieving statement, "Okay," and then asks a question, "But...?"

 **Questions give you control. Questions demand answers. Answers require thought.**

Your "okay, but..." causes your customers to reveal their true objections.

I saw this work magic recently. Shannon, an art consultant, spent 45 minutes with a client. They narrowed the choice down to a small original oil painting about 24" x 36". The client appeared to love the painting and offered no objections.

The price of the painting was $3,500 and Shannon's commission was 10%. Shannon definitely wanted the commission. She felt sure her client wanted the painting. She was excited.

They were sitting comfortably in the "viewing room" admiring the painting, when the client suddenly said, "I need to think about it. I'll be back."

After 45 minutes of "selling" and hearing no objections, Shannon felt the temptation to "bear down," and push for the sale, or to "bail out" and hope her client would return.

Instead she said, "Okay, but I've found that when someone really needs to think about a piece of art, then it *might not* be the *perfect* piece. What *might not* be *perfect* about this piece?" She shut up. Her client paused, then he said, "It's not big enough."

Later Shannon told me that she almost "fell out of her chair." She wondered why a client would admire a piece of art for 45 minutes that wasn't "big enough."

If she had let him leave to "think about it," the painting never would have become "big enough."

Once Shannon knew her client's true objection, she took action. She asked him, "How big do you want it?" He said, "Six feet by 53 inches."

Shannon was again shocked, but asked, "Why would it have to be that big?" He answered, "I'm Robert Rines, and I took a world-famous photograph of the Loch Ness creature. I want to commission a painting of Nessie to hang in the National Inventors' Hall of Fame in Akron, Ohio."

Thinking she had lost the sale, Shannon's natural curiosity was aroused and she gently asked, "What was your interest in this smaller painting?"

 **"Curiosity is far more important than knowledge ..."** Albert Einstein

Mr. Rines went on to say that he had already commissioned a well-known artist in Scotland to paint the piece but that he really liked the style of this local Hawaii artist, Thomas Deir.

Shannon told him that the artist might be interested in painting the piece. She arranged for Mr. Rines to have dinner with Thomas Deir and the art gallery owners.

The dinner led to a $100,000 painting and a trip to Scotland for Thomas Deir. Shannon's $350 commission became $10,000. **It was easy.**

The client won. The art consultant won. The artist won. The art gallery won. It was: **"win/win/win/win."** Why? Because the art consultant got *curious*. She said, "Okay, but..." She discovered the true objection, then overcame it.

"Bailing out," or "bearing down" would have caused her client to leave the gallery, probably never to return.

When your customer says, **"I'll be back,"** say, "Okay, but are you *sure* this is the one you want?"

 **Make the "okay" statement, follow it up with the "but" question, and the truth will emerge.**

When you ask, "Are you *sure* this is the one you want," and your customer says, "No," as many will, it means that you may not have found the right item yet. You can then ask, "What's not *perfect* about it?" Be *curious*.

When your customer answers, "Yes, I'm sure it's the right one," say, "Okay, I'll wrap it up and have it ready when you return. How are you going to pay for it?" Shut up!

Make the sale or get a deposit.

Companies have different policies on accepting deposits, or setting merchandise aside. Follow your company's policy, but make the sale. Ask for the money.

Customers expect to pay for what they buy.

 **Customers who will not give you their money have not bought your merchandise.**

Discover the truth. **It's easy.**

When you get a **price objection**, say, "Okay, but... is the price your *only* objection?"

Price objections come in many forms. You might hear: "It's too much," or "It's more than I want to spend," or "It's beyond my budget," or "I think I can get it cheaper somewhere else," or "Wow!"

"Sticker shock" paralyzes some customers. When you hear, "It's too expensive," say, "Okay, but is the price your *only* objection?"

 **Make the "okay" statement, then ask the "but" question.**

Shut up and let your customer answer. Many times the answer will be "No." Some customers offer price objections when the truth is they don't like it enough to buy it.

 **If your customer doesn't like your product enough to buy it, *any* price is "too much."**

You must discover the *true* objection before you can overcome it. When you say, "Okay, but is the price your only objection?", and your customer says, "No," you should ask, "What *else* is not perfect?"

When you say "perfect," your customers know that you are concerned about *their satisfaction,* not *your sale.* You make the "trust sale."

When your customer says, "Yes, price is my only objection," ask "If I could make you feel better about the price, would you buy it today?" If your customer answers, "No," to this question, you still may not have discovered the *true* objection. Ask, "What else *might not* be *perfect?*"

You must discover the truth, and the whole truth, before you can proceed.

When you ask, "If I could make you feel better about the price, would you buy it today?" and your customer answers, "Yes," you are moving towards the sale. Now you must make your customer *feel better* about the price.

Making your customer *feel better* about the price does not necessarily mean you have to discount or lower your price.

Some companies allow and even encourage discounting to close a sale; some do not. In either case, your first attempt should be to justify your existing price.

 **To make your customers *feel better about the price*, emphasize your product's quality, uniqueness and/or workmanship.**

Tell your customers *why* it is expensive. Customers need to know that your prices are fair. Say: "We sell the highest quality products. The store owner would rather have me respond to your price objections here in the store than have you deal with dissatisfaction later. Cheaper isn't always better."

When artist Thomas Deir was negotiating with Robert Rines, price became an objection.

Mr. Rines said, "The artist in Scotland will only charge me $40,000." Thomas Deir said, "Then you have an easy decision to make. Do you want a $40,000 painting or a $100,000 painting?

Robert Rines knew what he wanted. He paid the price. He *got* what he wanted.

When you have sufficiently justified your price and your customers ask for a *discount*, handle the request in one of two ways:

1. If you *cannot* discount, explain why in such a way that you make the sale anyway.

2. If you *can* discount, get a commitment for the purchase before agreeing to the discount.

If you are asked to discount the price, but you are not allowed to, then say, "We do not discount because we feel that every customer should pay the same price; the fair price. To allow discounting we would have to inflate our prices. Customers who didn't ask for discounts would be paying too much."

 **Many people who ask for discounts do not need a discount to buy. They just want a discount *if* one is available.**

When you explain *why* you do not discount, your customer may say, "Okay, it doesn't hurt to ask," then buy at your regular price.

If your store has multiple locations you might say, "We don't discount because we have several locations and want to offer the same prices to everyone. Rather than inflate our prices and discount, we lowered all of our prices to the lowest possible price. This makes it fair for everyone." Add: "So, if price is your only objection, you should buy it, because the price is fair." Shut up!

My purpose is not to suggest discounting. I support the golden rule of retail: "The person with the gold makes the rules." Store owners decide how to price, market and sell their merchandise. Be prepared for success, whatever your store rules are.

If your store encourages discounts and your customer requests one, then ask, "If I *could* get you a discount on that item, *would* you buy it?" If you get a "No," why offer a discount? Instead ask, "What else is not perfect?" Always determine the *true* objection before attempting to overcome it.

When you ask, "If I *could* get you a discount *would* you buy it?", and your customer answers, "Yes," ask, "How are you going to pay for it?" Shut up and wait for the answer.

 **A customer who won't agree to pay for your product is not ready to buy it.**

When you ask, "How are you going to pay for it," and your customer says, "I'm going to write a check," say, "Okay, the authorized discount is 10%; the total with tax is only $5,342." Shut up!

Customers will use many other excuses. The specific merchandise you sell will determine the specific objections you will hear. Script your own "okay buts," then rehearse them.

 **The motto of the Boy Scouts and Girl Scouts is: "Be Prepared." Be prepared for the excuses you know you will hear.**

If your customer wants to know the discount, ask, "If you are pleased with the discount, are you prepared to buy?" If your customer says, "Yes," state your policy and expect the sale. Say, "If I can get you the maximum 10% off, will you buy it today?"

Some excuses are common to all retailers; others are too specific and too numerous to mention. All excuses can be handled with the "okay, but ..." philosophy. Find a way to say: **"It's okay not to buy, but tell me why."**

Remember: the *true* objection is one of three:
1. "I don't like it enough to buy it."
2. "I don't have enough money to buy it."
3. "I like and want it, but need more assurance that it's *okay* to buy it."

When you make the "okay" statement and ask the "but" question, the #3 customer will hesitate. This customer cannot give you a specific reason for not buying it. There isn't one.

When you ask, "What's not perfect?", this customer might say, "Nothing really. I'm just not sure."

You have now gained permission to "nudge." It's the next step to making **retail selling easy**.

Chapter 10

Selling Decisions

Decide: "To bring to a definitive end..."
WEBSTER

Step #7 — Nudge

Webster defines a *nudge* as a "gentle push." Your customers sometimes need a "gentle push" to make a buying decision.

Nudging your customers should be done only when you are *sure* they want the product.

People don't mind being nudged in a direction they *want* to go.

You should only nudge after your customer assures you that the product is *perfect*.

Let's say your customer tells you, "I want to think about it." You respond with, "Okay, but I have found that when someone needs to think about it, it might not be the *perfect* item. What might not be *perfect*?" Your customer answers, "Well, nothing really, it's not that... I like it, I just need to think about it."

Get curious, be an "objection detective." Look for the truth, discover the real objection, if there is one. When you learn that there is no true objection *then* you can *nudge*.

Take the pressure off, and seek the truth. Say, "Okay, but let's think about it further while you are still in the store. Let's try to be *sure*. What about the color: Is the color perfect, or is there something about the color that bothers you?" Shut up - observe - mirror.

Select one feature of the product, distinguish it, question it, try to find fault with it. If you discover a problem, solve it and make the sale.

When your customer assures you that the color is perfect, identify another feature and repeat the process.

 **As your customers assure you that each feature is *perfect* they sell themselves in the process. It becomes "okay" to buy.**

Next, say, "Okay, the color is perfect. What about the size?" (then the fit, the shape, the model, the feel, the texture, the height, the length, the width, the style, the designer, the artist, the composition, anything else, and lastly, the price?)

If everything is perfect, ask, "Are you confident that you're getting a good value for your dollar?" This is your final question.

After asking your final question, shut up. If your customer answers, "No," to this question, then you've traveled a long distance to finally arrive at the *truth*. Go back to step #6 and overcome the price objection. Do not *nudge*.

On the other hand, when a customer answers, "Yes, I'm sure the price is fair," then it's time to nudge.

Take control, sum it up for your customer, make the sale. Say, "Okay, the color is perfect, the fit is perfect, you like the style and shape, it feels good and you're comfortable with the price. It sounds *perfect*. I suggest you get it now. You're here now, I'm here now, it's *perfect* now, it will be *perfect* from now on." Shut up!

 ***Silent* pressure forces your customers to make a decision: yes, or no. Either one is okay.**

Customers say: "I want to think about it" to avoid making a decision. Eliminate that option. It's okay for your customer to say, "No," but find out *why*. It's also okay to say, "Yes."

Sometimes your customers need to hear: "Go ahead and get it." They respond with, "Yeah, you're right. Okay."

An insincere or premature nudge can backfire. You must be *sure* that your customer likes, wants, needs, can afford, and is willing to buy your merchandise *before* you nudge.

Let's say your customer is looking at a dress. She decides not to buy it. She doesn't like it because it makes her look too short. She tells you, "I want to think about it." It would be premature to say, "Go ahead and get it." The truth is still hidden. She needs a different dress.

When you search for imperfection and discover it, back off and solve the problem. You may have to go back to step #5 and show a different product. You probably have lots of choices.

 **Your search for imperfection sells your customers on *you*.**

When you look for genuine reasons *not to buy* you assure your customers that *your goal* is *their satisfaction.*

Your customers discover that you wouldn't encourage them to buy something unless it was *perfect*. You make the "trust sale." You make the product sale. **It's easy.**

Many times your product *is perfect*. The color is right, the fit is great, the style is ideal, the price is affordable, everything is *perfect,* but your customer isn't ready to say, "Yes." It's time to *nudge.*

 **When your customers won't say no, get them to say yes.**

When you nudge and shut up, it's your customer's move. The silent pressure is on.

You both agree that it's *perfect.* You say, "Go ahead and get it," and shut up. Your customer thinks: "Should I or shouldn't I?" Stay focused, stay quiet, look at the merchandise, let the silent pressure work for you.

Your customer can take the pressure off by buying it, or by giving you a good reason for not buying it. In either case, you both win. You make the sale, or you discover the true objection, and then you make the sale. **It's easy**.

Script and rehearse your nudges. Some nudges are more appropriate in some stores than others. Some nudges are more appropriate with some customers than with others. Some nudges are more comfortable for some salespeople than others. Some nudges are:

Price Nudges:
"It's worth it."
"It will pay for itself."
"You only pay for it once."
"It's only money."

Satisfaction Nudges:
"You'll be glad you got it."
"You'll love it forever."
"It will last you a long time."
"It will give you continuous pleasure."

Urgency Nudges:
"Now is the time to get it."
"Go ahead and get it."
"Do it now."
"Go for it."
"We are running out of these." — (must be true)
"The sale ends soon." — (must be true)
"You can only get it in our store." — (must be true)

Ego Nudges:

"You'll get many compliments on this."
"You'll get lots of attention."
"Your friends will be impressed."
"It's one of a kind."
"It's you."
"You'll be the cat's meow."

Guilt Nudges:

"You deserve it."
"Treat yourself."
"You owe it to: her, him, them, or yourself."
"He, she, or they — owe it to you."
"I want you to have it."

Vacation Nudges:

"It's okay; you're on vacation."
"You'll remember your vacation every time you look at it."
"Buy it with vacation money."

Question Nudges:

"Why not?"
"Is there a good reason for not getting it?"
"Are you sure you like it?" (If the answer is yes, say, "Then get it!")
"Is this the one you like the best?" (If the answer is yes, say, "Then get it!")

The *real selling* is done during steps #5, #6 and #7: — Giving information, overcoming objections, and nudging. This is what distinguishes *salespeople* from cashiers, clerks, and order takers. *Salespeople* give information, overcome objections, and nudge. They also keep selling after the customer says, "Yes." It's the next step in the system.

Chapter 11

Selling More

Step #8 — Add On

I walked into an ABC convenience store looking for bottled drinking water. I knew what I wanted, and found it easily. I selected my favorite brand of water and placed it on the counter.

The salesperson looked at me and asked, "Would you like some fresh fruit to go with your water?" I instinctively answered, "No, thank you," but I immediately looked around to see the fresh fruit. I didn't know ABC sold fresh fruit. I *was* a little hungry.

The cashier observed my response, and waited quietly. I spotted some bananas, and said, "Don't ring it up yet. I want a banana." She said, "They are all the same price. Pick the biggest one."

I randomly selected a banana and put it next to my bottle of water. She looked at my banana, walked over to the fruit counter and returned with a different banana and said, "This one is bigger." I bought both bananas.

The two bananas cost more than the bottle of water. She doubled the sale at the register; I enjoyed eating both bananas. **Win/win.**

The very next day I walked into a different convenience store to get another bottle of drinking water. The cashier was chit-chatting with a fellow employee. I put my bottle of water on the counter and waited.

In a few seconds — which seemed like an eternity— the cashier turned from her co-worker and walked toward me.

She looked directly at the bottle of water, and without looking at me went straight to the cash register, rang it up and told me what I owed.

As I started to pay I spotted some bananas on the counter. I thought, "Hmmm, those look good." I *was* a little hungry.

I could "feel" the cashier "tapping her toe," impatiently waiting for me to pay for my water and leave. I did; still hungry. **"Lose/lose."**

Both convenience store employees had exactly the same opportunity. One seized it, one missed it. Both convenience stores are in good locations, they both have good merchandise. Both stores are paying someone to do the same job. One is a *salesperson,* one is a *cashier.* One doubles sales, one rings up sales.

 **Salespeople are a retailer's greatest asset. They determine the success or failure of a business.**

Here is another example of how to add-on. I was in Bill Wyland's office at his north shore art gallery. My back was to the showroom.

Bill's attention kept shifting to the gallery behind me. Suddenly, he stood up and walked to the front door just in time to meet a customer who was leaving.

Bill had been studying a sale being made behind me. A client was buying a framed, limited edition lithograph. It was $1,600. The client wrote a check, and was leaving. Bill sensed that something was missing. He took action.

Bill introduced himself to the client, complimented him on his selection, and asked, "Did you see the matching table for that piece?" The client looked surprised and said, "No, is there a matching table?"

They walked back into the gallery and Bill showed him the table. The client loved it and asked, "How much is it?" Bill said, "That's the best part of all. It's an artist's proof, and it's only $16,000." Silence! Pressure! Kaboom... Kaboom... Kaboom...

The client eventually spoke and said, "There is no way I could pay $16,000." Bill said, "Okay, but do you like it?" The client said, "I love it." Bill asked, "Did my salesperson explain our financing program to you?" The client said "No, I paid cash. How does your financing program work?"

Once the client understood the financing option he financed the $1,600 painting *and* the $16,000 table, *and* kept his cash. **It was easy.** "Win/win."

The original salesperson was satisfied with the $1,600 sale, and his $160. commission. Bill Wyland is *never* satisfied.

Bill followed the system, and made a $16,000 add-on, and the $1,600 commission.

Hopefully, Bill's salesperson learned a valuable lesson. Bill's client will definitely enjoy his table for the rest of his life. **"Win/win/win."**

Bill returned to his office, shook his head and said, "It makes me wonder how many sales we miss."

 **Money is easier to spend when you're looking at it.**

Supermarkets and other retailers display "impulse items" at the cash registers. Customers buy the magazine or candy that they had ignored or rejected moments ago while shopping.

Shoppers count their change and look around for something else to buy. They think, "If there is anything else I need, I should get it now." People using a credit card know they only have to sign it once regardless of how many items they buy.

Recognize the golden opportunity right in front of you when customers give you their money. You have obviously made the "trust sale," now start selling more merchandise.

It works! It works with bananas, it works with art. It works with anything. **It's easy.**

I went into a major department store to buy a suitcase. I found the luggage section and began looking around for help. I tracked down a "clerk." She answered my questions and I said, "I'll take it."

I handed the clerk my credit card and she headed for the register. I headed for the display of luggage accessories. I felt a sense of urgency. I thought, "If I want something else, I better find it before she starts ringing up the suitcase." I almost said, "Don't ring it up yet," but I wasn't sure if I wanted anything else. Stress!

My stress, and the store's additional opportunity ended when I heard the cash register go: "Ka-ching ka-ching ka-ching." I stopped looking at the accessories and waited to sign the voucher. I signed it and left without buying accessories. **"Lose/lose."**

When I handed the salesperson my credit card she should have taken it and said, "Feel free to look around. I'll hold on to your card." I would have said, "Thank you," relaxed, and looked around for something else to buy.

As I looked at the display of accessories I could have asked questions. Better yet, she could have pro-actively given me information about accessories, and maybe doubled her sale and my pleasure. It could have been **"win/win."**

Add-on when you *see* the money. When the credit card, cash, or checkbook comes out, sell more — add-on. **It's easy.**

 **When the customer, the merchandise, and the money are all in front of you, think: "What else do I sell that this customer could use?"**

Before ringing it up, ask yourself three questions.
1. "Who is my customer?"
2. "What is my customer buying and why?"
3. "What else do I have for my customer?"

Ask yourself, *"What's the deal here?"* Get curious. Is your customer:

A mom buying something for her daughter?
A husband buying something for his wife?
A wife buying something for her husband?
A couple buying something for their home?

Determine what else you sell that might suit this customer, then pro-actively suggest it.

Your pro-active trigger words are: "Oh, by the way..." Say, "Oh by the way, we have:

A pair of shorts to match the T-shirt.
A ring to match the pendant.
A painting to match the sculpture.
A rug to match the curtains.
A shirt to match the tie.
A pot to match the pan."

After you say, "Oh, by the way..." and suggest something, *shut up, observe* and *mirror*.

When your customer looks in the direction of something you suggested, go get it, call for it, send for it, or direct your customer to it, but above all, sell it. **It's easy.**

Chapter 12

Selling Friendship

Step #9 — Befriend

"He who has a thousand friends has not a friend to spare, and he who has one enemy shall meet him everywhere."

EMERSON, CONDUCT OF LIFE

Befriending starts after the sale, not before. Too many salespeople try to *befriend* their customers before the sale. They may make friends and lose sales.

The best time to "get personal" with your customers is when you are ringing up the sale, processing the credit card voucher or obtaining check approval.

Look for your customers' names on credit cards and checks, and call your customers by name.

There is nothing sweeter than the sound of hearing your own name.

Community Selling

If you recognize your customer, look at his or her name on the check and say, "It's always nice to see you, Mr./ Mrs. Johnson. Thank you for shopping with us today. Please come back soon."

If you don't recognize your customer ask: "Is this your first time in our store?" or "Are you a regular customer?" Find out, then act appropriately.

 **A new customer at your register represents future sales.**

The last impression you leave is an important part of the overall first impression you make. Make first and last impressions that encourage your customers to return to your store and refer their friends.

Get to know your regular customers. They will ensure your ongoing success. Look for common bonds and mutual interests. Say something positive about your customer's child, spouse, car, hobby or life that demonstrates your interest.

Become aware of local events that might interest your customers. Mention the high school or college football game, the school carnival, or a new movie.

Yes, I'm condoning, and even recommending, "small talk." But, only while *completing* the sales transaction.
Never make "small talk" prior to the purchase, or at the expense of your next customer.

 **As your customers leave your store, sell the return visit.**

For example, you might say: "I'm sure that dress will get you a lot of compliments. Stop back and tell me what people say."

Use your head; ask yourself: "What does my customer want to achieve with my product?" Then, wish your customer success, and request feedback — because you care. **It's easy.**

Many people stand in line at the bank hoping to get a particular bank teller to handle their transactions. Why? It's because they like the service and personal attention they know they will get from that teller.

Your favorite bank teller doesn't offer you a discount or higher interest rate than the other tellers. He or she just makes you feel happier... or more important.

Likewise, your customers will return to your store rather than to your competition for the same reason. You're giving them first class service, and boosting their ego too.

 **A solid base of return customers makes retail success easy.**

People buy gifts all year long to honor birthdays, anniversaries, events and holidays. Discover the future needs of your customers while they are in your store. They will remember you when it is time to buy that gift.

Resort Selling

Retailers in resort areas rely on tourists for their customer base. Most tourists don't "come back." Tourists have busy schedules and you may get only one chance to be with them in your store. Make it count.

You *can* befriend and sell the return to many of your tourist customers. The same rule applies as when befriending local customers: **Befriend at the end.**

When you accept a check or credit card from tourist customers, notice their name and where they live. Tourists love to talk about "back home."

You may know someone who lives in their area, or maybe you have visited their town or state. Notice where people live, and call them by name. Make a positive *last impression*. It sets you up to sell the return.

Say: "Thank you, Mr. Smith. I see you live in Colorado. It must be beautiful there this time of the year."

Ask: "Are you here on vacation or business?"

Ask: "What do you enjoy doing when you are away from home?"

Tourists cherish inside information from locals about where to go, what to do, where to eat, and what to buy.

Show genuine interest in your tourist customers. Find out what they like, then help them find it. If they like a particular cuisine, recommend a restaurant.

If you have a friend who works at a restaurant (most people living in resort areas do) send your customer to your "friend's table." Set your customer up for a special experience. Ask your customer to return and tell you how the dinner was.

When you discover that your customer likes to sightsee by car, you can recommend a route to take and places to stop along the way.

Again, you do all of this while ringing up the sale, not while selling. This conversation fills a silent void, and sells the return. It completes the system. It works. **It's easy**.

Chapter 13

Selling Success Traits

*People say: "He's a natural-born salesman." or
"She has the gift of gab."*

People are no more "born" salespeople than they are doctors, lawyers or any other profession. Salespeople are *developed*, not born.

*A*nyone can *learn* to sell, yet there are certain traits that will ensure greater selling success. You can develop these traits and improve them.

I created a list of "Selling Success Traits" from a "Gallery of Superstars;" the 10 best salespeople I've ever known. I listed the traits that make them "great."

Some of these superstar salespeople possess unique, individual talents that aid in their selling success, but are not crucial to it.

For example, some people are funny. People like someone who can make them laugh. Yet when people who are not funny try to be, it backfires. You must be yourself. Use the tools you possess.

Other salespeople are quick-witted. They play "mental combat" with their customers and like to win. They always know what to say, and when to say it. This too is a tough trait to *teach*.

Some salespeople are overbearing, and pressure customers into buying. This is not necessarily a *positive* trait that everyone should try.

The traits I looked for in my "Gallery of Superstars" were those traits common to all 10 of them. I asked myself, "What do these people have in common that makes them so successful at selling?"

My list included men and women of differing ages, different nationalities, and varied educations. Some had sales experience. Some didn't.

I concluded that age, gender, nationality, education and work experience were non-factors when determining someone's potential success in selling.

I also observed that many companies (while they won't admit it) stress the importance of a person's age, gender, nationality, education and work experience. It's illegal to discriminate, but it's common. It's also counter-productive.

People are also guilty of *self-discrimination*. Many people limit their potential success and blame their failure on their age, gender, nationality, education or work experience.

As I consider my "Gallery Of Superstars" I see people similar to *you* in age, gender, nationality, educational background and work experience.

You too can be a successful salesperson if you possess, and continue to develop, these 10 traits.

Selling Success Traits	**Score (1-10)**
1. Enthusiastic	_____
2. Honest	_____
3. Focused	_____
4. Positive	_____
5. Goal Oriented	_____
6. Disciplined	_____
7. Reliable	_____
8. Clean	_____
9. Healthy	_____
10. Knowledgeable	_____
Total Score	_____

As you consider each of these traits, score yourself on a 1-10 scale for each trait. Total your score. If your score totals 100, it means that you consider yourself perfect in all 10 traits. If so, you should get another opinion.

Self-analysis can be less than objective. Ask your friends or your boss to grade you on these 10 traits, and compare their score to yours. It may be revealing.

Consistently seek to improve yourself in all 10 of these traits. As your total score improves, so will your total sales, self-esteem and success. **It's easy!**

Selling Success Traits

Enthusiastic — Enthusiasm sells. Enthusiasm is contagious. Enthusiastic salespeople radiate confidence and trust.

The most effective enthusiasm is *bridled*. When you are so excited that you can hardly contain yourself, but do, you have *bridled* enthusiasm.

Your enthusiasm makes the "trust sale," which leads to the product sale. Your enthusiasm for your product says "You can trust me."

For example, if you *knew* that the merchandise you are selling is likely to be returned the next day because it's defective, overpriced or misrepresented, how *enthusiastic* would you be while selling it? Think about it.

Enthusiasm is not a flamboyant display of fancy adjectives describing your product. Enthusiastic people are often seen as being extroverts. The truth is, many are just the opposite. Some very successful, enthusiastic salespeople, entertainers and artists are introverts. They like being alone.

When "on stage" however, these introverts are enthusiastic. They are excited about their craft or art. They know how to play the part.

Get excited about what you are selling, *be enthusiastic*. You are "on stage" when you are selling. Your customer is your audience. Play the part, *be enthusiastic* — **it's easy.**

Years ago, I gave "enthusiasm lessons" to myself and my salespeople. I studied enthusiastic people and asked myself, "How are they acting that makes them appear to be enthusiastic?"

I analyzed enthusiastic behavior. I analyzed my own behavior when I became enthusiastic about anything. I developed a simple formula for enthusiasm. **It's easy.**

When you are with a customer:
1. Talk just *a little bit* louder than *you* normally do.
2. Talk just *a little bit* faster than *you* normally do.
3. Open your eyes just *a little bit* wider than *you* normally do.
4. Smile just *a little bit* more than *you* normally do.

Imagine this: You find a paper bag in the street. Inside you discover $1,000 in small, unmarked bills. You take the bag home and describe your find to a friend. You will be:
1. Talking a *lot* louder.
2. Talking a *lot* faster.
3. Your eyes will be *wide* open.
4. You'll be grinning *ear to ear.*

Why? Because you are excited! Practice these four acts, and you'll be constantly enthusiastic and excited about your merchandise.

Honest — The truly "great salespeople" always speak the truth. They do not exaggerate the truth or invent it.

Unfortunately, some people believe that selling means saying what the customer wants to hear. Not true. Selling is giving factual information.

Salespeople who *make up* facts forget what they say, and find themselves in trouble with contradictions. The truth never changes. You will always remember the truth.

Customers often ask questions that salespeople can't answer. The honest salesperson makes the sale by saying, "That's a good question. I don't know the answer, but I'll find out."

This response proves to the customer that the salesperson can be trusted. The "trust sale" is made. The product sale is made. Be honest. **It's easy!**

Focused —The "great ones" always remember *why* they are *where* they are. They keep their mind and body together.

 Some sales people bring their bodies to the store, but allow their minds to go back home… or somewhere else.

Focus your attention on the opportunity before you. When customers are in the store, the "great ones" are focused on their customers.

You bring about what you think about. Some salespeople are *in the store,* but thinking about something else such as:

> What's for dinner tonight?
> What's on TV tonight?
> What am I doing this weekend?
> How much longer before I can go home?
> Will I get that date?

I've witnessed some salespeople in the store, being paid, while:

> Reading books.
> Talking on the telephone.
> Doing crossword puzzles.

Eating.

Visiting friends.

Visiting co-workers.

Staring into space.

Whenever you catch yourself wondering what you should be thinking about, look at your feet, and then get your mind in sync. If your feet are in front of a customer, your mind should be on the customer.

If your feet are under the dinner table, get your mind on your food. You'll have better digestion. If your feet are propped up in the sand, framing the sunset, get into that.

Positive — Successful salespeople *expect* success. They think about their *good* customers. They anticipate more of them. They find them.

Refuse to listen to negative stories from other salespeople or merchants. Leave your personal problems at home. Recite positive affirmations. Tell yourself: "This is going to be a great day."

Goal Oriented — Great salespeople have hourly, daily, weekly, monthly and yearly goals. They know where they are going. They figure out how to get what they want.

If your store or company gives you goals to reach, achieve them. If not, set your own.

You should know your average *sales per hour* and have goals to increase it. The "great ones" are constantly pursuing a new *personal best*. They target on achieving their best day, best week, best month and best year.

 **You will subconsciously drive yourself toward the goals you set.**

Why do so many people fail to succeed? They fail to analyze where they are going, and consequently fail to get there.

If you are failing to plan,
you are planning to fail.

Disciplined — The "great ones" don't take short-cuts. They follow a system. They put pressure on the system to get results rather than putting pressure on themselves or their customers.

The "great ones" follow the rules. They abide by store policies and dress codes. They institutionalize their success. **They make success easy.**

Reliable — My "Gallery of Superstars" never miss a sales shift. You can count on them to arrive early for work, and leave late. They willingly attend sales meetings and training classes. They consistently produce results. **They make their success easy.**

Clean — The "great ones" always look their best. They are aware of the importance of first impressions. They dress to impress their customers, not co-workers or friends.

Great salespeople are immaculate. Their hair is neat, fingernails are trimmed and clean, shoes are shined — nothing is overlooked.

The importance of dress and grooming was discussed in Chapter Four. It is repeated here because the "great ones" validate it.

Healthy — Why do healthy people sell more? It's simple. They feel better, look better, have more energy and miss less, if any, work. It's hard to sell when you're sick; it's impossible when you're home in bed.

Staying healthy is easy. Too many people aren't.

Being healthy is simple:
1. Watch what, and how much, you eat.
2. Get sufficient sleep.
3. Avoid tobacco, alcohol and drugs.
4. Get some exercise.

Knowledgeable — The "great ones" *know their stuff.* They are knowledgeable. Gaining knowledge requires time and study. The "great ones" take the time to study, but they also have great results *immediately.*

Every sales company has seen a new salesperson, with very little specific knowledge, step onto the sales floor and outsell the "old pros" that have been there "forever."

How can this be? It's simple: When a customer meets a salesperson who is enthusiastic, honest, focused, positive, goal oriented, disciplined, reliable, clean and healthy — the "trust sale" is made — the product sale is made.

As you gain knowledge your results will improve further.

To be sure you appreciate the importance of these 10 traits, imagine the opposite. How would you rate the potential success of a salesperson who was: dull, dishonest, distracted, negative, lost, undisciplined, unreliable, dirty, sickly and ignorant?

Give yourself a "checkup from the neck up" at least once a month. Look into the mirror and give yourself a 1-10 score on all 10 success traits. Total your score. Pick your weakest trait and work to improve yourself.

Make these traits dominant; you *will* sell *more*. **It's easy!**

A **Success Traits Scoresheet** is printed at the end of this book to make it easy for you to use. I grant you permission to copy the **Success Traits Scoresheet.**

Chapter 14

Selling Habits

Habit ... "A behavior pattern acquired by frequent repetition..." Webster

Any act repeated over and over becomes easier and easier. When you acquire successful selling habits your selling success is easy.

 **As the steps of Pro-Active, No-Pressure Selling become habitual, so does your success.**

You will automatically behave in a way that is now comfortable, habitual and successful.

When customers enter your store, imagine it is your job to place them on a "railroad track" that goes to "Sale City."

Once you get on a railroad track, you will go where the track goes, *provided* you:

1. Stay on the track.
2. Keep moving.

You may move at different speeds, but you *will* arrive at your destination.

Imagine the nine steps of Pro-Active, No-Pressure Selling as the track to "Sale City." Record you progress. Here's how:

THE SALE CITY EXPRESS

– Example –

CUSTOMERS	Greet 1	Position 2	Speak 3	Tell 4	Show 5	Overcome 6	Nudge 7	Add-On 8	Befriend 9	$ Total
1	✓	✓	✓	✓	✓	✓	✓	✓	✓	$100
2	✓	✓	✓	✓	✓			✓	✓	$80
3					✓			✓	✓	$50
4	✓	✓	✓					✓	✓	$70
5								✓		$10
6	✓		✓	✓	✓	✓	✓		✓	0̶
7	✓	✓	✓	✓	✓	✓			✓	$80
8	✓	✓	✓	✓						0̶
9						✓	✓	✓	✓	$40
10	✓	✓	✓	✓	✓	✓			✓	$90
Totals	7	6	7	6	7	5	3	5	9	**$520**

Retail Selling Made Easy © Success Dynamics, Inc. • Honolulu, Hawaii 1966

When your customer *leaves* your store, take a minute and analyze *your* behavior. Check off the steps you took to "Sale City."

After documenting your behavior with at least 10 customers, grade yourself on a 1 – 10 scale. How many times did you:

1. Greet
2. Position
3. Speak
4. Tell
5. Show
6. Overcome
7. Nudge
8. Add-on
9. Befriend

Next, add up your total sales to these 10 customers. Compare your *results* to the 10 prior customers, and so on.

Set goals to improve your *score* on any of the nine steps. Set goals to increase your *sales* to your next 10 customers.

You will notice that as you get higher scores on the nine steps you will have more sales. You will now have successful selling habits.

 **You control sales by controlling your behavior.**

Many salespeople "take a minute" and analyze their *customer's* behavior. They think things like: "cheapskate, time-waster, jerk," etc.

When describing customers who buy, salespeople say, "Nice people." Many salespeople change their opinion of the customer from "jerk" to "nice person" the second the customer says, "Okay, I'll take it."

Salespeople are fickle. It's easy to like customers who buy, and tempting to scorn those who don't.

Your customer's personality, appearance or behavior is not as important as **your attitude**. You had a "jerk" in your store; so what? "Jerks" buy too. What's most important is how you worked with the "jerk."

Another label for a "jerk" might be "testy." Some customers are "testy." They also test *you*. When you pass their test they buy, and vice versa.

 **You pass your customer's test when you stay on the "Sale City Express."**

When customers are greeted, welcomed, put at ease, given information, assisted in their buying decisions and invited to return — they buy, return, and refer their friends. **It's easy.**

When your customer leaves the store ask yourself nine questions, and record your answers on the "Sale City Express."

The "Sale City Express" is printed at the end of this book to make it easy for you to use. I grant you permission to copy the "Sale City Express."

Nine Question Review

1. Did I greet this customer?
2. Did I position myself properly with this customer?
3. Did I ask this customer if he or she had been in the store before?
4. Did I give this customer a verbal tour of my store?
5. Did I pro-actively give this customer specific information when needed?
6. Did I overcome any objections that were offered?
7. Did I nudge if appropriate?
8. Did I add-on at the register if a purchase was made?
9. Did I befriend my customer in a way that he or she is likely to revisit my store?

Lastly, record the sale total even if it was a zero.

You will discover that you don't always need all nine steps, but you still follow the track. Some customers don't make excuses, so step #6 is not necessary. Some customers don't need a nudge. A train doesn't always make every stop, but it does *stay on the track.*

Your goal is to get to "Sale City." If skipping a step is necessary or appropriate, that's all right; skip it, but stay on the track. Take the next step.

 **The track determines the direction; the customer determines the speed and number of stops. Be sensitive.**

Salespeople derail themselves whenever they ask, "How are you today?" Their customers say, "Fine; how are *you?*"

This track leads to "Small Talk City." The further down the track to "Small Talk City" you go, the harder it is to get back on track to "Sale City."

Don't "throw switches" on yourself that derail you. When your customer "throws a switch" on you, politely "throw the switch" back to the Sale City track.

For example, you say, "Hello." Your customer responds with, "Hi, how are you today?" Say, "Great, welcome to the store. Have you been in before?"

The customer "threw the switch" to "Small Talk City"; you politely switched it back to "Sale City."

Some customers "throw the switch" to "No Sale City." They declare: "I'm just looking!" If you don't get back on the track, this customer will take a "self-guided tour" to "No Sale City."

Nathan is a salesperson in an import furniture store. He told me a story about the first time he used the "Sale City Express" to control his behavior. His story offers a great example of how this tool works.

A customer entered Nathan's store. Nathan said, "Hello." The man cordially returned the greeting, then walked away from Nathan.

Nathan positioned himself properly and asked, "Have you been in our store before?" The customer replied, "No, I haven't."

Nathan proceeded to give him the "verbal tour," then disengaged and invited him to look around and ask any questions he might have.

Nathan wandered back to his sales counter and began checking-off his progress on the "Sale City Express." He thought, "Okay, I've completed steps #1, #2, #3 and #4; what's next?" The "Sale City Express" said: "Show." Nathan looked up at his customer, and saw he was looking closely at a small wooden hutch.

Nathan re-approached his customer and offered specific information about the hutch. He described its design, features, benefits and workmanship. His customer appeared to like the hutch, but said, "I need to think about it."

Nathan stayed on track. He said, "Ok, but I've found that when someone needs to think about it, sometimes it's not the perfect piece. What *might not be perfect* about this hutch?"

The customer turned quickly, looked directly at Nathan and barked, "I just need to think about it!"

Right here is where many salespeople might think, "What a jerk." They might walk away, and *never* re-approach that customer. They would fail the "jerk test."

Nathan *was* shocked. He told me that he hustled back to the safety of his sales counter thinking, "I didn't know there were land-mines on the "Sale City Express."

Nathan stood behind his counter, shaken by his customer's abusive response. He looked up at his customer and noticed that he was still eyeing the hutch.

Nathan began to wonder; "What should I do now?" He looked down at his "Sale City Express" and it said: "Nudge."

Nathan froze. The *system* was saying: "Your customer is still interested in the hutch. He has received sufficient information to make his buying decision. You have given him the opportunity to walk away, reject it, or find fault. He hasn't. **Nudge!**"

Nathan's *feelings* said: "No way!" *Fear* was controlling him.

Nathan stood there watching his customer look at the hutch. He soon realized that if he did *nothing* (as his feelings dictated) his customer would walk out the door. He decided to take action.

Nathan walked up to the customer, with his knees knocking, and timidly said, "I see you're still looking at this hutch. It must be the right one." The customer instantly looked at Nathan and said, "You're right, I'll take it."

Nathan walked back to his counter, still shaking. The customer handed Nathan his credit card. Nathan looked down at his "Sale City Express" and saw: "Add-on." He froze: fear.

Nathan couldn't bring himself to suggest the lamp or table that matched the hutch. He also realized that if he had not forced himself to nudge, he would have missed that sale. If he attempted to add-on, he might have sold the lamp or table too.

Following the system allows you to overcome fear and stay on the track to Sale City."

Chapter 15

Selling With The Boss

"We shape our tools and then our tools shape us."
THOREAU

Ralph Waldo Emerson observed that all he needed was someone to get him to *do* what he *could do*. Most people are *capable* of doing more than they *do*. Bosses get employees to *do* what they *can do*.

Of all the decisions made in a retail business, the most important one is made by your customer: "Buy it, or not!"

The next most important decisions are made by you. *You decide* if, how and when to talk to your customer. *You decide what to say,* and *how to act.* These important *decisions* affect the all-important customer decision: "Buy it, or not?"

If your boss was watching you and expecting you to follow all nine steps of the Pro-Active, No-Pressure Selling System, *you would,* wouldn't you? Of course you would.

Too few bosses observe their employee's behavior this closely. As a result, most retail salespeople are alone with most of their customers.

With the absence of a physical boss, your habits become the boss.

 **You do what is habitual, right or wrong — IT'S EASY.**

Habitualize behavior that leads to success. Continuously using your "Sale City Express" will help you develop "success habits."

 **Preparation + Opportunity = Success**

Every customer walking through the door represents opportunity for you. *Be prepared.* No one can accurately pre-judge or measure each opportunity.

Did you see the movie "Pretty Woman"? It illustrates the danger of pre-judging customers, even in a posh Beverly Hills boutique.

If you *could* accurately judge the potential of every customer on sight alone, you could *adjust* your behavior to *match* the opportunity.

Airlines have a first class section. Everyone sitting in first class gets "first class treatment." They didn't all buy a first class ticket. Some are using free upgrades. They don't all *look like* first class passengers, but they all *get* first class service. So should your customers.

 **When your customers enter your store, they enter your "first class section."**

Customers *choose* to enter your store. Be honored. They deserve first class treatment. *Give* it to them. They will *give* you their business.

Let's say your boss just explained the importance of following the Pro-Active, No-Pressure System and told you not to take any short cuts. Your boss then said, "Okay, pretend I'm a mouse in the corner today. I'm going to watch every move you make, and listen to every word you say to your customers. I'm going to take notes and review them with you at the end of the day."

You say, "Why are you doing that?" Your boss says, "I want to be sure all customers get what they need and deserve. It will help. You will sell more, and make more money than you would if I stayed in the back-room and ignored you."

What a boss! Success is pleasing your boss. Don't let the ambition, priorities or personality of your *store* boss limit your success. Become your *own* boss — the *real* boss.

When you become your *own boss*, and truly want success, you will please the boss. *You will give yourself success.*

In selling, you must specify a *sales amount* that represents success. How much do you need to sell today, this week, and this month to be successful? Make these numbers important.

Unfortunately, some retailers do not share the sales results of their stores with their employees. This is a mistake.

Keeping sales a secret robs the company of the opportunity to hold the staff accountable for sales results and denies opportunities to build teamwork.

 **When owners share numbers with salespeople, their salespeople can be held accountable for those numbers.**

Retailers that provide their salespeople with specific daily and monthly goals are on the road to success.

Your *store* boss may not give you a goal. Your *real* boss — you — may have to provide it. The goal will keep you focused on *giving* first class treatment to every customer. That's the best way to reach the goal. First class customer service results in first class sales results.

 **To stay focused on your ideal behavior, face "the real boss." Your *results* are "The Boss."**

Your thinking affects your behavior. Control your behavior by controlling your thinking. You bring about what you think about.

 **When you think about success, you bring about success.**

In another of my books, "Success Made Easy," I devoted several chapters to demonstrating how to put **"The Boss"** to work for you and achieve any goal in life.

"The Boss" becomes a "mind-trigger." It's a visual tool that keeps you focused on your goal. Without this control, your mind may wander to some other aspect of your complex life while customers are in your store.

As a salesperson, your primary goal is to maximize sales and hit store goals.

First, establish a monthly sales goal for yourself. Consider your past performances, and the results of your colleagues. Also consider current conditions in your life.

Next, ask yourself, "How much *can I* sell this month?" Stretch yourself slightly.

 **When you reach for the stars you don't get any mud in your hands.**

Set a monthly goal that's not *too hard*, nor *too easy*. You must believe in your potential to succeed. Next, divide your monthly goal by the number of days you plan to sell this month. This gives you a daily goal.

 **A person without a goal is like a ship without a rudder.**

Now, employ **"The Boss."** Start with the graph on side **A**. (see page 139 figure 1)

Next use side **B** (see figure 2, page 140) the same as you would a savings account. Sales are like deposits; your accumulative sales total is like your bank balance.

"The Boss" is also printed at the end of this book to make it easy for you to use. I grant you permission to copy **"The Boss".**

"The Boss" lets you know how you're doing. **It's easy.**

Figure 1 — Example ▶

NAME: KAY

(#1) Establish sales goal —
(Example here is $38,000)

(#2) Create a scale with some room to exceed your goal —
(Example here is $50,000)
Divide your goal by 10 to evenly spread the scale.
(Example here is $5,000 each)

(#3) Create a track line from 0 to your goal at end of the month. (Example here is $38,000)

(#4) Create a trail —
This is your actual accumulated sales for the month —
(Example here is $10,334 in five days. Almost $5,000 ahead of the track.)

Make dots and draw lines to continue the trail.
Do it everyday. Keep the trail ahead of the track, and you are on the trail to success. **It's easy.**

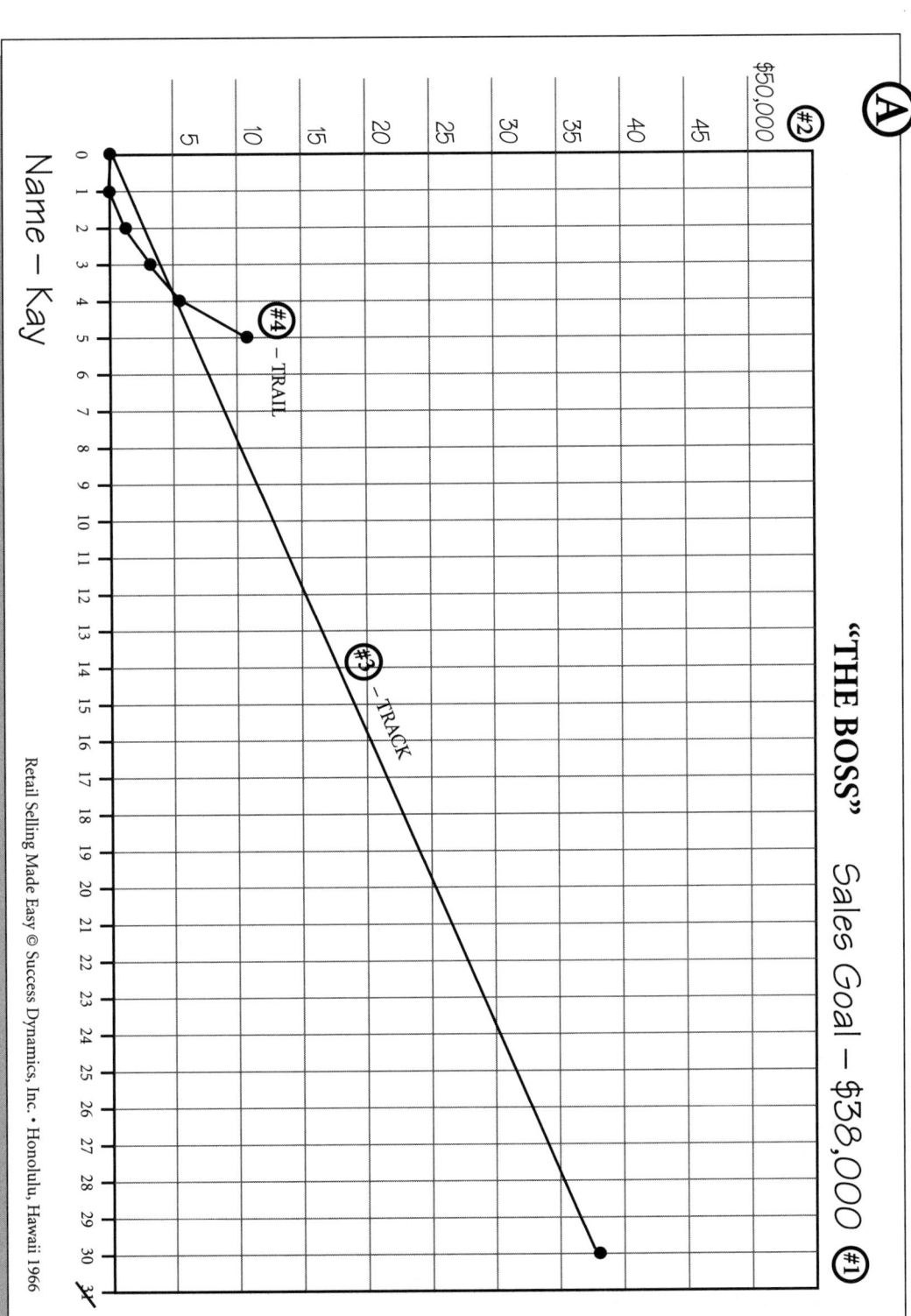

"THE BOSS"

NAME: KAY   Goal $38,000

Daily Sales

1. _____ OFF _____
2. _____ $ 1630 _____
3. _____ 1804 _____
4. _____ 2200 _____
5. _____ 4700 _____
6. _____
7. _____
8. _____
9. _____
10. _____
11. _____
12. _____
13. _____
14. _____
15. _____
16. _____
17. _____
18. _____

Accumulative Sales

1. _____ 0 _____
2. _____ $ 1630 _____
3. _____ 3434 _____
4. _____ 5634 _____
5. _____ 10,334 _____
6. _____
7. _____
8. _____
9. _____
10. _____
11. _____
12. _____
13. _____
14. _____
15. _____
16. _____

Figure 2 — Example ▲

 Enter your daily sales total.

 Add today's total for accumulated sales total.

Transfer accumulated total to side **A**. (The Trail)

Retail Selling Made Easy © Success Dynamics, Inc. • Honolulu, Hawaii 1966

"THE BOSS"

NAME: KAY Goal $38,000

	Daily Sales		Accumulative Sales
1.	OFF	1.	0
2.	$1630	2.	$1630
3.	1804	3.	3434
4.	2200	4.	5634
5.	4700	5.	10,334
6.	1998	6.	12,332
7.	OFF	7.	
8.	OFF	8.	
9.	SICK	9.	
10.	SICK	10.	
11.	2151	11.	14,483
12.	SICK	12.	
13.	2086	13.	16,569
14.	OFF	14.	
15.	OFF	15.	
16.	1382	16.	17,951
17.	2154	17.	20,105
18.	3656	18.	23,761
19.	3036	19.	26,797
20.	1545	20.	28,342
21.	OFF	21.	
22.	OFF	22.	
23.	4748	23.	33,090
24.	2102	24.	35,192
25.	3214	25.	38,406
26.	2700	26.	41,106
27.	4510	27.	45,616
28.	OFF	28.	
29.	OFF	29.	
30.	2204	30.	47,820
31.		31.	

Figure 3 — Example ▲

Here you see Kay's "challenge" as she was ill on the 9th after 2 days off. She was "out of the game" for ten days, but still ended up a *winner* thanks to **"The Boss."**

Figure 4 — Example ▶

Kay sells in a small retail bikini store in Waikiki. You can see how **"The Boss"** kept her on track all month, to reach her monthly goal of $38,000.

Kay's sales caught up with the track on the 4th. A big day on the 5th put her ahead of the track.

Kay had a difficult time from the 11th to the 17th due to illness. But, using **"The Boss"** she put herself back on the track to success with a total $47,820 in sales for the month.

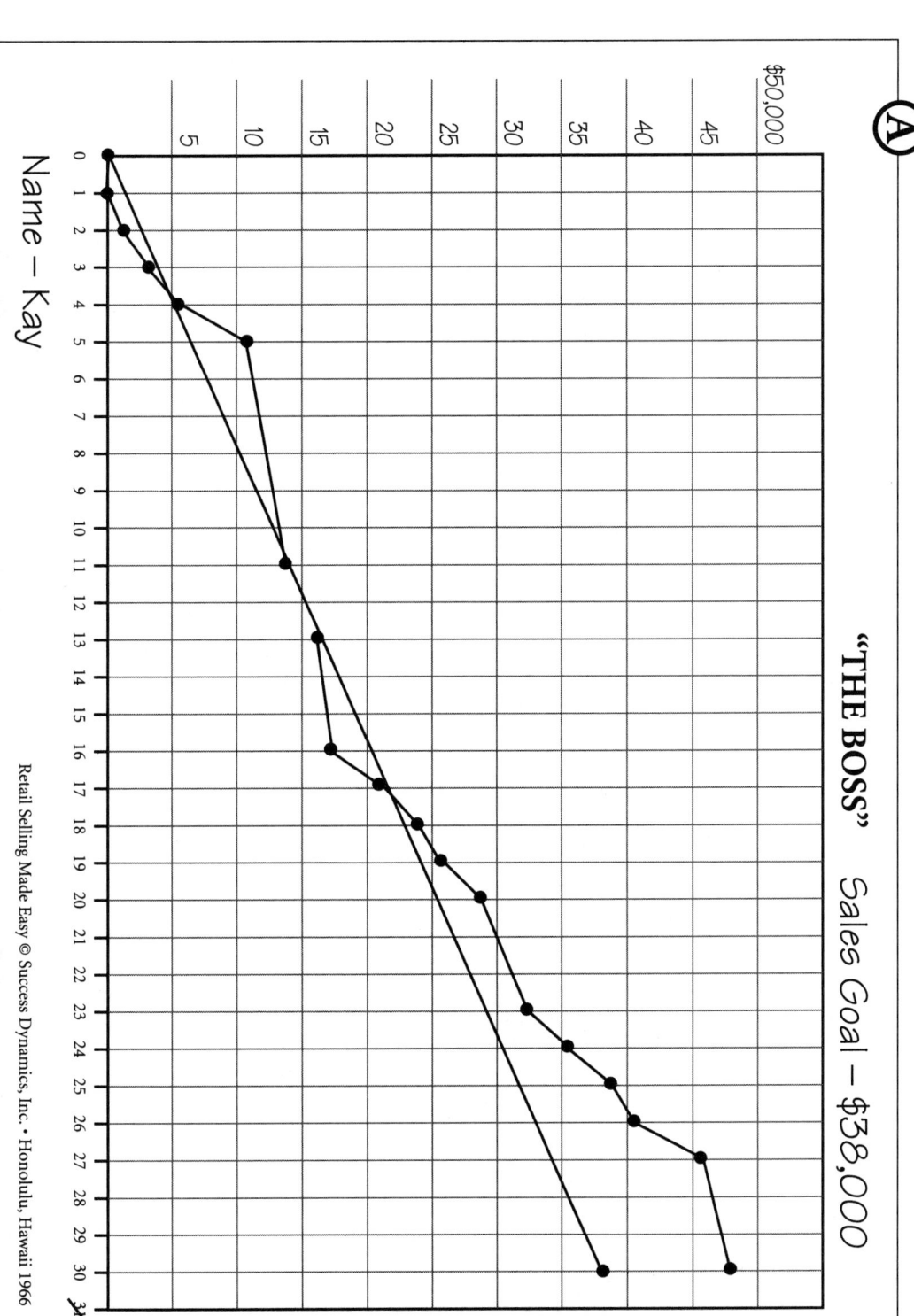

Chapter 16

Selling Success

Success is:
1. "Satisfactory completion of something . . .
2. The gaining of wealth and fame . . .
3. One that succeeds . . ."

WEBSTER

Webster wraps it up. Complete your job and you will gain wealth, fame and success — **It's easy.**

This book gives you a system to follow. Add a touch of common sense as you follow this system, and **you will succeed.**

Following any system requires discipline until it becomes a habit. Stay on the course and accept nothing less from yourself than success.

 **The time required to succeed is exactly the same as the time needed to fail — 24 hours a day.**

Always think positively and focus on success. Be aware of your *thinking* both on and off the selling floor. It determines your future.

Stay out of the "loser's lounge." Shield yourself from negative stories peddled by disgruntled and pessimistic employees or merchants.

Accept no excuses for failure other than your own behavior. You have full control over your own behavior. Choose successful behavior and you will succeed. **It's easy.**

Refuse to quit. See *minor* setbacks and obstacles as just that, *minor*. Life is a constant learning experience. Keep moving in a forward direction and you *will* make progress.

Keep your heart in the right place. Who you *are* speaks so loudly people can't hear what you *say*. Work *for* your customers, and success will work *for* you.

 **Your customers will enjoy your products longer than you will enjoy their money.**

This Pro-Active, No-Pressure Selling System is not on trial; **it works.** *Remember:* "It" doesn't work every time, but you can "work *it*" every time. When you do, "*it*" will work *for* you.

Be a *giver*. *Give* information, *give* service, *give* your time; your customers will *give* you their money. **It's easy.** "Give /Give —Win/Win."

Enjoy Success.

The End

Acknowledgements

Once again many generous people have helped me write a book. I thank them all.

Mahalo to:

Tom O'Gwynn – For exposing me to retail. I appreciate him every day.

Ruby Pollock – For her never-ending patience as I revised my changes over and over.

Doug Behrens – For turning my ideas into reality on both the inside and the outside of this book.

Kenny Williams – For "capturing the moment" on the cover.

Dick Lyday – For transforming another manuscript into boxes of books.

And to:

Rich Budnick – Becky Ehling – David Hagerman – Betty Ling – Ed Randolph – Ed Schneider – Brick Thompson
 for their editorial advice and assistance.

Mahalo also to the ever-growing list of companies that have allowed me to refine and prove this Pro-Active, No-Pressure Selling System.

Aloha Shells	Grande's Jewelry & Gems
Appliance Parts Company	Haleiwa Supermarket
Atlantis Submarines	Hawaii Prince Golf Club
Avalon Restaurant	Hawaiian Island Creations
BEBE Sport	HMSA
Big Save/Value Centers	Hollywood USA
BK Ocean Sports	Honolulu Book Shops
Black Pearl Gallery	Hyatt Regency Waikiki
Blue Ginger	Hilton Waikoloa
Body & Soul	Indich Collection
Crater Enterprises	Indo Pacific Trading Co.
Castle & Cooke-Retail	International Marketplace
Chaney Brooks & Co.	Kahn Galleries
Chocolates For Breakfast	Kauai Lagoons
Coconut Marketplace	Keahou Shopping Center
Collectors Fine Art	Kohala Kollection
Cosmic Candy & Popcorn	Koko Marina Shopping Center
Élan Corp.	Kona Inn Shopping Center
Endangered Species	Little Ceasars Pizza
Everything Moves Co.	Kramers
Fantasy Photo-San Francisco	Lahaina Hat Company
The Fun Factory	Lahaina Market Place
Fisherman's Landing	Lahaina Printsellers
Golden Reef Jewelry Store	Lahaina Scrimshaw

Lahaina Trader
Lanai Sportswear
Lanihau Center
Loco Boutique
Magnet 5-0
Martin & MacArthur
Maui Divers
Maui Outlet
Mauna Lani Bay Hotel
Nohea Gallery
Outrigger Hotels
Outrigger Shops
Splashin Fashions
Pacific Jewelry Design Center
Pai Moana Pearls
Paradise Cove Luau
Paul Brown Salon
Pictures Plus
Pier 39/San Francisco
Pier 39-One Hour Photo
Picture San Francisco
Poipu Bay Resort
Pomegranates In The Sun
Prima Classe
Prince Kuhio Plaza
Raging Isle
Regent Jewelers

Royal Hawaiian Shopping Center
Return To Paradise
Sea Life Park
Sgt. Leisure
Schuler Homes
Sultan Company
Surf & Sea Haleiwa
Simic Art Gallery
The Body Shop
The Pretzel Maker
The Wharf/Cinema Center
Today's Little People
Treasures Jewelry
University Imaging
Ward Centre
Ward Warehouse
Villa Roma
Waikiki Aloe
Waikiki Trader Corp.
Waimea Valley
Whalers Village
Windward Mall
Wyland Galleries Hawaii
Wyland Collection Stores
Wyland Studios USA
Xcel Wetsuits

Ordering Information

Success Dynamics, Inc.
P.O. Box 489
Haleiwa, HI 96712

Phone: (808) 637-5020
Fax: (808) 637-4914
e-mail: easy@aloha.net

Write, call, fax or e-mail us to request a current price list, or more information about these books:

Success Made Easy by Ron Martin

Retail Selling Made Easy by Ron Martin

Sales Management Made Easy by Ron Martin

Selling Success Traits

                                          Score (1-10)

1. Enthusiastic .... _____
2. Honest .... _____
3. Focused .... _____
4. Positive .... _____
5. Goal Oriented .... _____
6. Disciplined .... _____
7. Reliable .... _____
8. Clean .... _____
9. Healthy .... _____
10. Knowledgeable .... _____

     Total Score .... _____

THE SALE CITY EXPRESS

	Greet	Position	Speak	Tell	Show	Overcome	Nudge	Add-On	Befriend	$ Total
	1	2	3	4	5	6	7	8	9	$
1										
2										
3										
4										
5										
6										
7										
8										
9										
10										
Totals										$

CUSTOMERS

Retail Selling Made Easy © Success Dynamics, Inc. • Honolulu, Hawaii 1966

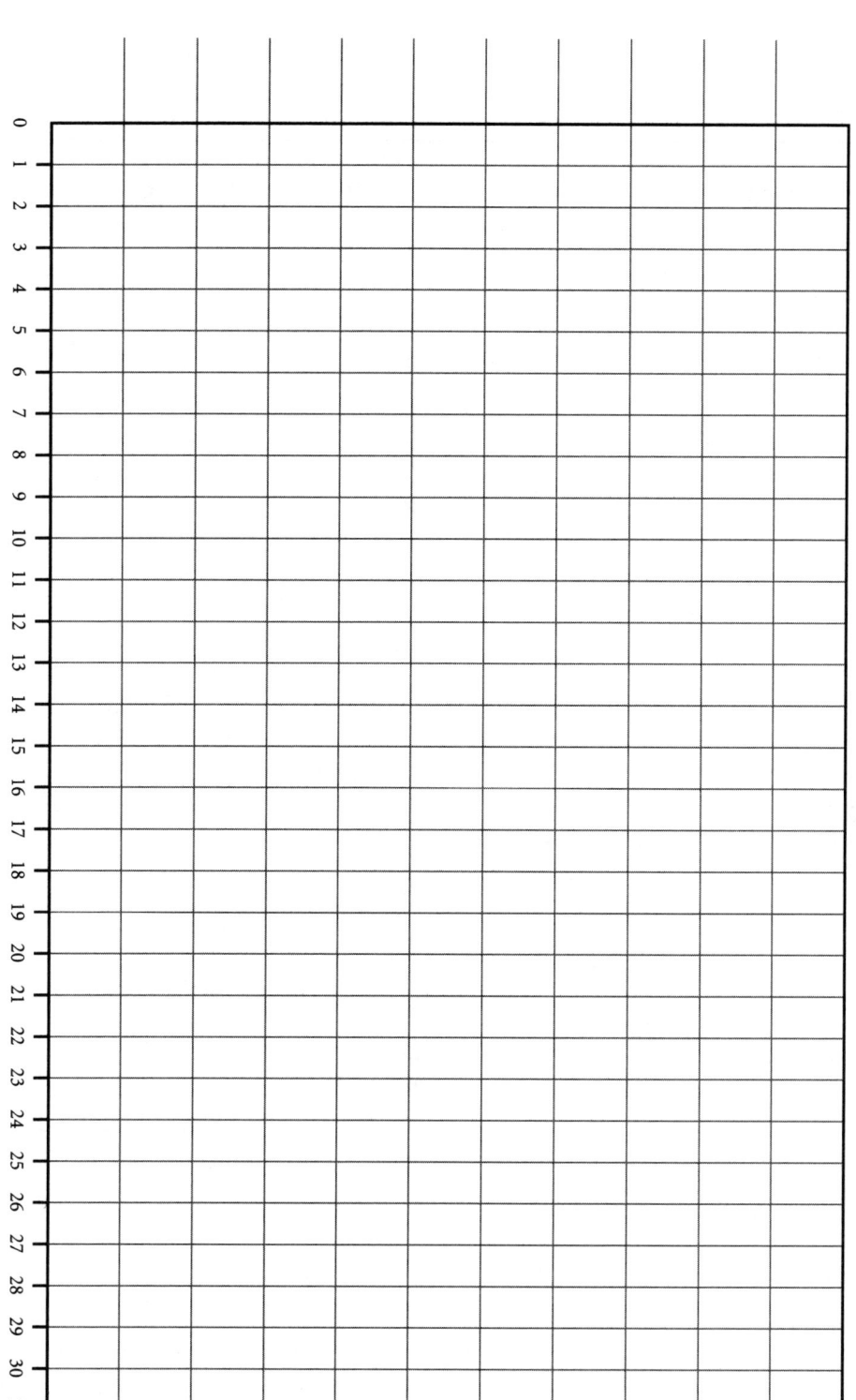

"THE BOSS"

NAME: _____

Daily Sales	Accumulative Sales
1. _____	1. _____
2. _____	2. _____
3. _____	3. _____
4. _____	4. _____
5. _____	5. _____
6. _____	6. _____
7. _____	7. _____
8. _____	8. _____
9. _____	9. _____
10. _____	10. _____
11. _____	11. _____
12. _____	12. _____
13. _____	13. _____
14. _____	14. _____
15. _____	15. _____
16. _____	16. _____
17. _____	17. _____
18. _____	18. _____
19. _____	19. _____
20. _____	20. _____
21. _____	21. _____
22. _____	22. _____
23. _____	23. _____
24. _____	24. _____
25. _____	25. _____
26. _____	26. _____
27. _____	27. _____
28. _____	28. _____
29. _____	29. _____
30. _____	30. _____
31. _____	31. _____

Retail Selling Made Easy © Success Dynamics, Inc. • Honolulu, Hawaii 1966